PLAY THE NOTEBOOM

Mark van der Werf and
Teun van der Vorm

CADOGAN
chess
LONDON, NEW YORK

First published 1996 by Cadogan Books plc, London House, Parkgate Road, London SW11 4NQ

Distributed in North America by Simon and Schuster, Paramount Publishing, 200 Old Tappan Road, Old Tappan, New Jersey 07675, USA.

All other sales enquiries should be directed to Cadogan Books plc, London House, Parkgate Road, London SW11 4NQ.

British Library Cataloguing in Publication Data
A CIP catalogue record for this book is available from the British Library

ISBN 1 85744 108 7

Typesetting by ChessSetter

Printed in Great Britain by BPC Wheatons Ltd, Exeter

CADOGAN CHESS SERIES

Chief Advisor: Garry Kasparov
Editor: Andrew Kinsman
Russian Series Editor: Ken Neat

Contents

Bibliography

The following books, periodicals and other resources were of particular use in the preparation of this monograph.

Books

Encyclopaedia of Chess Openings (ECO) Volume D
The Noteboom Variation (by Andrew Soltis)
The Complete Semi-Slav (by Peter Wells)
Secrets from Russia (by Mikhail Shereshevsky)
De eerste honderd jaren (Kroniek van het Leidsch Schaakgenootschap)

Periodicals

Chess Informant
New in Chess Yearbook
New in Chess Magazine
Die Schachwoche
Schaaknieuws
The Week in Chess [on the Internet] (by Mark Crowther)

Introduction

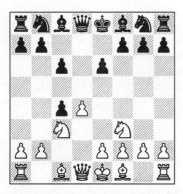

The Noteboom variation of the Slav Defence is one of the most underestimated variations in chess. For some reason it has had a bad reputation for a long time. Although lately the results for Black have improved, the popularity of **1 d4 d5 2 c4 e6 3 ♘f3 c6 4 ♘c3 dxc4!** is still not what it should be. This book will show that the Noteboom is a perfect addition to your repertoire, and we hope that it will help you to understand the positional and tactical ideas.

The Noteboom practically ensures an enjoyable game. It usually leads to an unbalanced position in which a short draw is very unlikely to occur, and is an opening for the adventurous player. He or she may be a tactical player or a positional player, but will certainly play chess for fun.

The Noteboom is sound. Recently White has been struggling to prove a tiny advantage. In most cases he does not succeed, and often fails even to obtain equality after the opening stage. It is not surprising that world-class players such as Kramnik, Sveshnikov and even Kasparov have played the variation.

Usually **4...dxc4!** will not come as a shock to your opponents. But the shock will be there after a while, when they try to remember the refutation and discover that there is none. Your opponent must play carefully just to regain his pawn and even if he succeeds you will have a good game. Your advantage is that you know the details and, more importantly, you understand the position.

The Noteboom is an unorthodox opening. Usually you play so many pawn moves that your opponent begins to think that he is playing a novice. However, the Noteboom, with its odd-looking moves, is powerful and will punish your opponent if he is not careful.

Why is it then that the Noteboom still has a dubious reputation? To find out the answer to that question we must turn back the clock a little.

The history of the Noteboom variation

The Noteboom variation is named after Dutchman Daniël Noteboom, who was the first player to regularly use **4...dxc4!** The games of Noteboom, who died in 1932 at the very young age of 21, contain many of the ideas that are used nowadays. The next game is a nice example of Noteboom's understanding of the position.

Voisin – Noteboom
Hamburg olympiad 1930

1 d4 d5 2 c4 e6 3 ♘c3 c6 4 ♘f3 dxc4 5 a4 ♗b4 6 e3 b5 7 ♗d2 ♗b7 8 axb5 ♗xc3 9 ♗xc3 cxb5 10 b3 a5 11 bxc4 b4 12 ♗d2 ♘f6 13 ♘e5 ♘bd7 14 ♕a4 0-0 15 ♘c6 ♗xc6 16 ♕xc6 e5 17 ♗e2 ♖e8 18 ♗f3 ♖c8 19 ♕a6

19...exd4 20 ♖xa5 ♘c5 21 ♕b5 ♘b3 22 ♖a2 ♖b8 23 ♕f5 dxe3 24 ♗xe3 ♘d4 25 ♕b1 b3 26 ♖d2 ♕a5 27 ♗d5 ♘c2+ 28

♔e2 ♕c3 29 ♖hd1 ♘xd5 30 cxd5 ♕c4+ 31 ♖d3 ♖bd8 32 ♔d2 ♖xd5 33 ♖xd5 ♕xd5+ 34 ♔c1 ♕c6 35 ♔b2 ♕f6+ 36 ♔xb3 ♘xe3 37 fxe3 ♖b8+ 0-1

At around the same time Englishman Gerald Abrahams also adopted this opening strategy and made his own substantial contribution to the viability of the Noteboom variation. Some opening books even refer to the variation as Abrahams variation, but we chauvinists stick to Noteboom. In this well-known game against Ragozin, Abrahams recovers from a poor position in the opening.

Ragozin – Abrahams
Great Britain-Soviet Union radiomatch 1946

1 d4 d5 2 c4 e6 3 ♘c3 c6 4 ♘f3 dxc4 5 e4 b5 6 ♗e2 ♘d7 7 0-0 ♗b7 8 d5 ♘c5 9 dxc6 ♗xc6 10 ♘d4 ♕d7 11 ♘xc6 ♕xc6 12 a4 ♖d8 *(D)*

13 axb5 ♕b7 14 ♕c2 ♘b3 15 ♖a6 ♘f6 16 ♗e3 ♗c5 17 ♗xc5 ♘xc5 18 ♖c6 ♘b3 19 ♗xc4 ♘d4 20 ♕a4 0-0 21 ♖a6 ♕b8 22 f4 g5 23 e5 ♘h5 24 g3 ♔h8 25 ♕d1 ♘g7 26 ♕g4 gxf4 27 ♕xf4 ♘df5 28 ♘e2 ♘h5 29 ♕e4 ♖g8 30 ♗d3 ♖g5 31 ♖c6 ♖d5 32 ♖fc1 ♔g7 33 b6 axb6 34 ♖c7 b5 35 ♖1c6 ♕d8 36 ♖c8 ♕a5 37 ♘f4 ♘xf4 38 ♕xf4 ♕e1+ 39 ♗f1 ♕e3+ 40 ♕xe3 ♘xe3 41 ♖d6 ♖gxe5 42 ♖xd5 ♖xd5 43 ♖c3 ♘xf1 44 ♔xf1 ♖d1+

45 ♔e2 ♖h1 46 ♔e3 ♖xh2 47 b3 ♖h5 48 ♖c7 ♖g5 49 ♔f4 ♖d5 50 ♔e4 h5 51 b4 ♖g5 52 ♔d4 ♖g4+ 0-1

Despite these games, the variation suffered from a bad reputation for a long time. Although black players soon discovered 15...e5! to counter White's pawn mass in the main line, they still had a hard time neutralizing the opponent's middlegame initiative. Our next game is a much-quoted example of the opportunities for White in the Noteboom variation. The powerful passed c-pawn supported by a typical breakthrough proves to be decisive.

Kholmov – Bikhovsky
Moscow 1967

1 d4 d5 2 c4 e6 3 ♘c3 c6 4 ♘f3 dxc4 5 e3 b5 6 a4 ♗b4 7 ♗d2 a5 8 axb5 ♗xc3 9 ♗xc3 cxb5 10 b3 ♗b7 11 bxc4 b4 12 ♗b2 ♘f6 13 ♗d3 ♘bd7 14 0-0 ♕c7 15 ♖e1 0-0 16 c5 ♘e4 17 ♕c2 ♕c6 18 ♕e2

♗a6 19 ♗xa6 ♖xa6 20 d5 exd5 21 ♘d4

21...♕a8 22 ♘f5 ♘df6 23 c6 ♖e8 24 f3 ♘c3 25 ♗xc3 bxc3 26 ♘d4 ♖b6 27 ♕d3 ♖b4 28 ♖ec1 a4 29 ♖xc3 ♕a5 30 c7 ♖c4 31 ♖xc4 dxc4 32 ♕xc4 ♖c8 33 ♘b5 ♘e8 34 ♕g4 ♕a6 35 ♕d7 ♔f8 36 ♖d1 a3 37 ♘d6 ♕xd6 38 ♖xd6 ♖xc7 39 ♕d8 a2 40 ♖d1 ♖b7 41 ♕d3 1-0

It was not until the early 1990s that Russian players rediscovered the Noteboom, and so began a remarkable revival with strong novelties and impressive results for Black.

Janakiev – Sherbakov
Mladenovac open 1994

1 d4 d5 2 ♘f3 c6 3 c4 e6 4 ♘c3 dxc4 5 e3 b5 6 a4 ♗b4 7 ♗d2 a5 8 axb5 ♗xc3 9 ♗xc3 cxb5 10 b3 ♗b7 11 bxc4 b4 12 ♗b2 ♘f6 13 ♗e2 ♘bd7 14 ♘d2 0-0 15 ♗f3 ♗xf3 16 gxf3?! ♕c7 17 f4 a4 18

d5 exd5 19 ♖g1 dxc4 20 ♘xc4 a3 21 ♗xf6 ♘xf6 22 ♕d4 ♖a6 23 ♘d2 ♖b8 24 ♔e2 ♖d6

25 ♕e5? ♖e8 26 ♕g5 ♖xd2+ 27 ♔e1 g6 28 ♕xf6 ♕c2 0-1

Recent results in the main variation have been so good for Black that many white players have turned to obscure variatons or even avoided the Noteboom variation altogether. Where do these successes come from? In order to understand that we will now focus on the most important positional and tactical characteristics of the Noteboom variation.

Positional themes

If you look at the diagram which starts this introduction you will notice that Black is a pawn up. In many variations White will not get his pawn back. Black can simply defend his weak pawn on c4 with ...b5, and if he is able to keep the pawn on c4, his queenside

structure is a valuable possession. The next game is a perfect example, in which Black maintains his queenside pawns and uses them to good effect.

Lin Weiguo – Stangl
Beijing 1995

1 d4 d5 2 c4 e6 3 ♘c3 c6 4 ♘f3 dxc4 5 a4 ♗b4 6 e4 b5 7 ♗e2 ♘f6 8 ♗g5 ♘bd7 9 0-0 h6 10 ♗xf6 ♘xf6 11 axb5 ♗xc3 12 bxc3 cxb5 13 ♕b1 a6 14 ♘d2 0-0 15 f4 ♗b7 16 ♗f3 ♕c7 17 g3 ♗c6 18 e5 ♘d5 19 ♗xd5 ♗xd5 20 ♘e4 ♖fb8 21 ♘c5 a5 22 g4

22...b4
What a triumph for the black queenside army! White cannot do anything to stop it, because the bishop on d5 controls the centre and prevents any aggressive activities.

23 ♖a2 ♕e7 24 h3 bxc3
Finally Black decides to break his pawn chain, as the a-pawn will bring victory in a few moves.

25 ♕c1 ♖b3 26 ♖c2 a4 27 ♖xc3 ♖xc3 28 ♕xc3 a3 0-1

Game 12, featuring Tregubov with Black, is another perfect example of this typical Noteboom strategy.

In nearly all Noteboom variations, Black has the advantage on the queenside. In some lines he is a pawn up, while in others, the main line for example, material is equal, but Black has two passed pawns. The next fragment shows some tactical and positional aspects of the 'Noteboom twins' on a5 and b4.

P.Cramling – Gdanski
Osterskars 1995

1 d4 d5 2 ♘f3 c6 3 c4 e6 4 ♘c3 dxc4 5 a4 ♗b4 6 e3 b5 7 ♗d2 ♗b7 8 b3 a5 9 axb5 ♗xc3 10 ♗xc3 cxb5 11 bxc4 b4 12 ♗b2 ♘f6 13 ♗d3 ♘bd7 14 0-0 ♕c7 15 ♘d2 e5 16 ♖e1 0-0 17 ♘f1 ♖fe8

This position also arises in game 24. In that game Black seized the advantage after 18 f3 e4 19 ♗e2 exf3 20 gxf3 ♘h5!

18 ♘g3
White decides to keep her kingside intact, but allows a strong advance.

18...a4!
Black puts his twins on the same rank, controlling three squares deep into White's territory. The move is based on a tactical trick: 19 ♖xa4 ♕c6 picks up a rook because the queen also threatens to give mate on g2. Note that a move earlier 17...a4 would have failed to 18 dxe5 and that after 18 f3 there is no trick at all.

19 ♖b1 b3?
Black was probably dreaming of pawns on a3 and b3 with this advance, but in fact Black's pawns now lose most of their power, because White can occupy the abandoned squares on a3 and c3. Black should, for instance, have played 19...e4 20 ♗e2 ♕a5 after which the pawns on a4 and b4 are a latent threat to White's position.

20 ♗a3
Now White can manoeuvre more easily and she eventually won after 20...g6 21 ♕d2 ♗a6 22 ♖ec1 h5 23 f3 ♕a7 24 ♕f2 ♖ac8 25 ♘f1 ♘f8 26 ♘d2 exd4 27 exd4 ♘e6 28 ♗b2 ♖ed8 29 ♖a1 ♘xd4 30 ♖xa4 ♖c6 31 c5 ♘e2+ 32 ♕xe2 ♗xd3 33 ♖xa7 ♗xe2 34 ♘xb3 ♘d5 35 ♘d4 ♖cc8 36 ♘xe2 ♘b4 37 ♗d4 ♖e8 38 ♘g3 ♖cd8 39

♗f6 ♖d2 40 ♗g5 ♖b2 41 ♘e4 ♘d3 42 ♖d1 1-0

In a typical Noteboom encounter White must decide the game early on, before Black reaches the endgame unharmed. He has some assets with which to build an attack, for example after 4...dxc4 White controls the centre and has more space, and if Black does not play carefully White's attack can suddenly become devastating. The next fragment features Kasparov in a simultaneous exhibition and if Kasparov has an attack ...

Kasparov – Tyomkin
Tel Aviv 1994

1 d4 d5 2 c4 e6 3 ♘c3 c6 4 ♘f3 dxc4 5 a4 ♗b4 6 e3 b5 7 ♗d2 a5 8 axb5 ♗xc3 9 ♗xc3 cxb5 10 b3 ♗b7 11 bxc4 b4 12 ♗b2 ♘f6 13 ♗d3 ♘bd7 14 0-0 ♕c7 15 ♘d2

15...0-0?
This move is logical but inaccurate. As games 24 and 25 show, Black should play 15...e5 in order

to restrain White's centre. See how quickly Kasparov's central pawns take up an ideal position.
16 f4!
That prevents the advance ...e6-e5 forever.
16...a4
Black has no counterplay in the centre and therefore switches to the queenside. He has to do something but his aggressive activities work like a boomerang.
17 e4?!
Premature. The notes to game 24 show two methods for White to achieve an overwhelming position here.
17...a3 18 ♗c1 ♖fd8?
Black should have attacked Kasparov's impressive pawn mass immediately with 18...♕d6. White's only move is 19 d5, after which 19...e5 creates a stubborn defence. Now Black's queenside counterplay vanishes as White occupies the weakness on b3.
19 e5 ♘e8 20 ♘b3

In a mere five moves White has made tremendous progress, and now he controls the entire board. Black therefore decides to sacrifice a pawn, but the complications prove to be in White's favor.

20...g6 21 ♕d2 ♗c6 22 ♕xb4 ♖db8 23 ♕c3 ♗xg2 24 ♔xg2 ♕b7+ 25 ♖f3 ♕xb3 26 ♕xb3 ♖xb3 27 ♗e4! 1-0

In this game Black committed suicide, but the next game shows the ideal strategy for White. First he uses his central pawn mass to cut Black's position in half and then he goes for the king.

Oei – Van Wissen
Leeuwarden open 1993

1 d4 d5 2 c4 e6 3 ♘c3 c6 4 ♘f3 dxc4 5 a4 ♗b4 6 e3 b5 7 ♗d2 a5 8 axb5 ♗xc3 9 ♗xc3 cxb5 10 b3 ♗b7 11 bxc4 b4 12 ♗b2 ♘f6 13 ♗d3 ♘bd7 14 0-0 0-0 15 ♕c2 ♕c7 16 ♘e5

16...h6?
White's last move is not without poison. In game 29 we show

that Black should not be afraid to sacrifice his h-pawn, which is quite a common theme in the Noteboom. After 16...♘xe5! 17 dxe5 ♘d7 18 ♗xh7+ ♔h8 Black has excellent compensation.

17 f4
Again this move secures an advantage for White. Now Black probably should not have taken the knight, but alternatives are hard to see.

17...♘xe5? 18 fxe5 ♘d7 19 ♖f4 ♗c6 20 ♖af1 a4
Finally Black puts his pawns to work but White has a more powerful specimen.

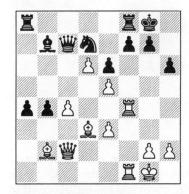

21 d5! ♗b7 22 d6
The end of the game is simple. Black can barely move, so White puts his heavy pieces on the kingside, and the decisive sacrifice is inevitable.

22...♕c8 23 ♕f2 ♕e8 24 ♕g3 g6 25 ♖g4 ♔h8 26 ♖h4 ♔g7 27 ♖hf4 ♔g8 28 ♖g4 ♔h8 29 ♕h3 ♔h7 30 ♕h5 ♔g7 31 ♖xf7+ ♕xf7 32 ♖xg6+ ♔h8 33 ♖xh6+ 1-0

The main line usually leads to a clash in the centre. At some stage White plays e4, creating an impressive centre and threatening e4-e5. Black must strike back immediately and play ...e6-e5 himself! Usually this advance is a pawn sacrifice but numerous examples show that capturing with dxe5 puts White in immediate trouble. The pawn structure after ...e6-e5 is so common to the Noteboom that we ought to spend a diagram on it.

The diagram position illustrates the character of the battle. White will try to use his influence in the centre to build a kingside attack, while Black tries to limit White's aggressive possibilities and will go for a queenside attack or an endgame. Virtually all endgames favour Black, because his queenside pawns become more powerful when there are fewer pieces left.

Understandably this structure is not very stable. If White does

not take on e5 then at some point Black can open the position with ...exd4. We will take a look at some examples with this pawn structure.

Llopis de Aysa – Yakovich
Seville open 1992

1 d4 d5 2 c4 e6 3 ♘c3 c6 4 ♘f3 dxc4 5 a4 ♗b4 6 e3 b5 7 ♗d2 a5 8 axb5 ♗xc3 9 ♗xc3 cxb5 10 b3 ♗b7 11 bxc4 b4 12 ♗d2?! ♘f6 13 ♗d3 ♘bd7 14 ♕b1 0-0 15 0-0 ♕c7 16 e4 e5

This is a common position in the Noteboom except for the bishop on d2 and queen on b1.

17 d5?!
An unusual but interesting move. White gives up the c5 square but gains some space and temporarily paralyses Black's bishop on b7.

17...♘c5 18 ♗e3 ♘fd7 19 ♘d2 ♖fb8?!
Black should have played 19...a4 immediately, since the bishop on

d3 prevents White from capturing the pawn on b4. After 20 ♗c2 ♕a5 Black's prospects are better.

20 ♗c2 a4

Now this move is harmless.

21 ♕xb4 ♗xd5

White has equalised easily. The game continues for some time but the outcome is already clear.

22 ♕a3 ♗e6 23 ♖fb1 ♕a5 24 h3 h6 25 ♔h2 ♕c7 26 ♔g1 f6 27 ♖xb8+ ♖xb8 28 ♖b1 ♖xb1+ 29 ♗xb1 ♕a5 30 ♗c2 ♔h7 31 ♔h2 ♔h8 32 ♔g1 ♔h7 33 ♔h2 ♕b6 34 ♔g1 ♔h8 35 ♔h2 ♔h7 36 ♔g1 ♗g8 37 ♔h2 ♗f7 38 ♔g1 ♗g8 39 ♔h2 ♗f7 40 ♔g1 ♕a5 41 ♔h2 ½-½

In this example White tried d4-d5 to keep the bishop on b7 out of play, but the knight on d7 gratefully jumped to c5 to control matters. The next game features dxe5, but not in a very good version.

Thieme – Van der Vorm
Leidschendam 1994

1 d4 d5 2 c4 c6 3 ♘c3 e6 4 ♘f3 dxc4 5 a4 ♗b4 6 ♗d2 b5 7 e3 ♗b7 8 axb5 ♗xc3 9 ♗xc3 cxb5 10 b3 a5 11 bxc4 b4 12 ♗b2 ♘f6 13 ♗d3 ♘bd7 14 ♕c2 ♕c7 15 h3 0-0 16 e4 e5 (D)

17 dxe5?

A clear mistake as the squares c5 and e5 soon become very weak.

17...♘h5

Heading for f4.

18 g3 ♘c5

This knight controls the important squares a4, e4 and e6. Now White plays a strange move that he cannot afford in this position.

19 ♘d4?! a4 20 0-0 a3 21 ♗c1 ♕xe5

Black has effortlessly regained the pawn and put his pieces on ideal squares. Note that Black now occupies the squares c5 and e5 which White controlled in the previous diagram. In such a position tactical possibilities appear from nowhere. In this position White cannot defend his knight and e-pawn. The rest is simple.

22 ♗e3 ♘xd3 23 ♕xd3 ♕xe4
24 ♕xe4 ♗xe4 25 g4 ♘f6 26 f3
♗d3 27 ♖fc1 ♖fc8 28 ♗d2 ♖ab8
29 c5 b3 30 ♘xb3 ♖xb3 31 ♖c3
♖xc3 32 ♗xc3 ♖a8 33 c6 a2 34
♖e1 ♘d5 35 ♗a1 ♖c8 36 ♖c1
♗b5 37 ♖c2 ♖xc6 38 ♖xa2 h6 0-1

In the main variation, ...e6-e5 is
Black's key move to keep some influence in the centre, but in other
lines Black often uses his extra c-
pawn to attack White's centre. But
the next fragment shows that playing ...c6-c5 does not automatically
solve all of Black's problems.

Tjiam – Van der Werf
Nijmegen 1993

1 d4 d5 2 c4 e6 3 ♘c3 c6 4 ♘f3
dxc4 5 g3 b5 6 ♗g2 ♗b7 7 0-0
♘d7 8 e4 ♘gf6 9 ♘h4 ♗e7 10 a3
0-0 11 f4

In this position Black is a pawn
up but White has some compensation. Black tries to free himself
but this is perhaps premature.

11...♕b6?!
Black wants to play ...c6-c5,
which is a good plan but only if
White cannot reply with d4-d5. A
better idea is 11...♘b6 12 ♗e3 ♕c7
intending ...a7-a6 and ...c6-c5 with
the d5 square sufficiently covered.
An attempt to attack immediately
with 12 f5 is totally ineffective after 12...c5.
12 ♗e3 c5?!
The natural follow-up, but it is
dubious.
13 d5!
Of course White does not allow
an exchange of pawns because his
d-pawn is more important than
Black's c-pawn.
13...exd5 14 exd5 ♖fe8
The alternative 14...♘e8 forces
some strong moves: 15 ♘f5 ♗f6 16
d6.
15 ♗f2 ♗f8?
Probably better was 15...g6 but
the attack will come anyway.
**16 g4! ♖ed8 17 g5 ♘e8 18
♕g4 ♘d6 19 ♖ae1 ♗c8 20 f5**
Black has a cramped position
and there is not much he can do
about White's attack. He therefore decides to do something with
his extra pawns, but it is to no
avail.
20...a5 21 ♕h5 b4 22 ♘e4 (D)
White directs his pieces towards
the black king. It is just a matter
of time before the decisive attack
starts.
**22...♖a6 23 ♗g3 ♘e8 24 d6!
♗xd6 25 g6 ♗xg3 26 gxf7+ ♔f8
27 fxe8♕+ ♖xe8 28 hxg3 ♕h6**

29 ♕xe8+ ♔xe8 30 ♘d6+ + ♔d8 31 ♘f7+ ♔c7 32 ♘xh6 ♖xh6 33 ♖e6 ♘f6 34 ♖c6+ ♔b8 35 ♖d1 1-0

16 ♖e1 ♕b7 17 ♖e2 ♗xd2 18 ♘xd2 ♖fc8

In this game ...c6-c5 was not enough to free Black's game. If White can play d4-d5 in reply to ...c6-c5 then perhaps Black should postpone ...c6-c5. However, if d5 is impossible then ...c6-c5 is an excellent move in most cases.

Delemarre – Sveshnikov
Tilburg 1994

1 d4 d5 2 c4 e6 3 ♘c3 c6 4 ♘f3 dxc4 5 e3 b5 6 a4 ♗b4 7 ♘d2 ♗b7 8 ♕f3 a6 9 ♕g3 ♘f6 10 ♗e2 0-0 11 0-0 ♘bd7 12 ♗f3 ♕b8 13 ♕h3 *(D)*
13...c5!
A strong move which gives Black a huge advantage, because 14 d5 ♗xc3 is impossible.
14 ♘ce4 cxd4 15 exd4 ♗d5
Black not only rids himself of his redundant c-pawn, but also gives White an isolated d-pawn and covers the all-important d5 square.

The result of the opening is clear. Black is a pawn up and has better positioned pieces. Sveshnikov does not let his prey escape.
19 ♖a3 b4 20 ♖ae3 ♘b6 21 ♘e4 ♘xe4 22 ♗xe4 ♗xe4 23 ♖xe4 ♕d5 24 ♗h6 ♕f5 25 g4 ♕g6 26 ♗c1 ♘d5 27 ♕g2 c3 28 b3 ♘f6 29 h4 h5 30 ♖f4 hxg4 31 ♖e1 ♖d8 32 ♔h2 ♖d5 33 ♖e5 ♖ad8 34 h5 ♕h6 35 ♖xf6 ♕xf6 36 ♗g5 ♕f3 37 ♕xf3 gxf3 38 ♗xd8 ♖xd8 39 ♔g3 ♖xd4 40 ♔xf3 c2 0-1

In these lines e4 is an important square. Black is willing to do anything to stop White from putting pieces or a pawn on that square. In some cases he is even willing to play ...f7-f5, weakening e5 but gaining total control over e4. Game 11 shows why this idea is valid.

Anti-Noteboom systems

White has several methods to avoid the Noteboom variation. These so-called Anti-Noteboom systems have their merits, but generally pose no serious problems for Black, though if you play the Noteboom you should study them thoroughly. The most dangerous line is the Marshall Gambit, in which White sacrifices a pawn in order to get a powerful initiative. This often leads to wild positions with Black's king staying in the centre for a long time, but the Noteboom specialist has no reason to fear this if he is properly prepared.

The most insipid line is the Exchange variation, which leads to a balanced position in which it is difficult for either side to play for a win. Although other setups to avoid the Noteboom create more tension than the Exchange variation, the character of these variations is positional rather than tactical.

About this book

Now you have seen some of the important strategical aspects of the Noteboom variation, and this book will further illustrate these ideas and introduce many more. It contains games rather than moves, because we feel that listing numerous variations does not contribute to a full understanding of typical positions.

The annotations contain ideas and variations. The former show the positional aspects, while the latter illustrate the ideas, show tactical possibilities and deal with some important alternatives in the opening.

Finally we hope you enjoy the book and, more importantly, enjoy playing the Noteboom.

Mark van der Werf
and
Teun van der Vorm
April 1996

1 White side-steps the standard 5 e3 and 5 a4

In order to avoid a theoretical battle in the main variation, white players have tried a number of different set-ups. None of these are really dangerous for Black, if he knows what he is doing. The most popular system is 5 ♗g5, covered in games 1 and 2, in which White tries to disturb the harmonious development of Black's pieces. In games 3-5 White plays a set-up with g3 and ♗g2 to quickly develop his kingside without trying to regain his c4 pawn. Recently White's results with this line have been fairly good, but Black should be able to equalize with precise play.

Game 1
Lukacs – Semkov
Vrnjačka Banja 1987

1	d4	d5
2	c4	e6
3	♘f3	c6
4	♘c3	dxc4
5	♗g5	

This move has become a popular way to avoid the main line of the Noteboom. Its main purpose is to disrupt the development of the black pieces. Two seldom seen alternatives are:

- 5 ♘e5 b5 6 a4 ♗b4 7 e3 ♗b7 8 ♕f3 ♕e7 and Black is fine.
- 5 e4 b5 6 e5 (6 a4 ♗b4 is game 6) 6...♗b7 7 ♗e2 ♘e7 8 ♘e4 ♘d5 9 0-0 ♘d7 resembles the Tolush variation of the Queen's Gambit Accepted. Black's chances are no worse.

| 5 | ... | f6 |

Black forces the bishop to retreat at the cost of a small weakening of his pawn structure. 5...♘f6 6 e4 b5 leads to the Botvinnik variation of the Slav Defence. With 5...♕c7 Black can avoid weakening his kingside, but this move allows White to take control over the centre (see game 2).

6 ♗d2 (D)

6 ♗f4 is played less frequently, but is by no means worse. For example: 6...b5 7 e4 a6 (alternatively 7...♗b4 8 ♗e2 ♘e7 9 0-0 0-0 10 a4 ♘g6 11 ♗e3 ♗xc3?! [11...♗b7? allows 12 axb5 ♗xc3 13 bxc6, but 11...♕d7 with the idea of 12...♗b7 and 13...♘a6 is interesting] 12 bxc3 a6 13 d5 exd5 14 exd5 ♕xd5 15 ♕xd5+ cxd5 16 axb5 ♗b7 17 ♖ab1

♘d7 18 bxa6 ♗xa6 19 ♖fd1 and in Dreev-Klinger, Palma de Mallorca 1989, White had sufficient compensation for the pawn in view of his pair of bishops and the poor positioning of the black pieces) 8 ♗e2 ♘e7 9 h4 ♗b7 10 h5 ♘d7 11 0-0 c5?! (Semkov suggests 11...g5 intending ...h7-h6 and ...♗g7, but 12 ♗d6 ♘c8 13 ♗xf8 ♔xf8 14 ♘h2 followed by ♘g4 and f4 leaves Black without counterplay; a more solid approach is 11...♘c8, 12...♗e7 followed by 13...0-0) 12 d5 e5 13 ♗e3 ♘c8 14 ♘h4 ♘d6 15 ♗g4 ♕c7 (15...b4 16 ♘a4 ♘xe4 17 f3 ♘d6 18 ♗xd7+ ♕xd7 19 ♘b6 wins the exchange) 16 ♗e6 0-0-0 17 ♕g4 and White was clearly better in Rajković-Semkov, Vrnjačka Banja 1987.

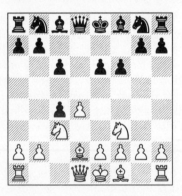

6 ...   a6!?
Black prepares ...b7-b5. The immediate 6...b5 gives White a direct target: 7 a4 b4 (7...♗b4?! 8 axb5 ♗xc3 9 ♗xc3 cxb5 10 b3 cxb3 11 e3 ♗d7 12 ♕xb3 a6 13 ♗a5 ♕c8 14 ♗b4 followed by ♘d2-e4-c5/d6 gives White good chances for the

pawn) 8 ♘e4 ♗a6 9 ♖c1 ♕a5 10 e3 c3 11 bxc3 ♗xf1 12 cxb4 ♕d5 13 ♘c3 ♕d7 14 ♔xf1 ♗xb4 15 ♘e4 ♗e7 16 g3 and White was better in the game Psakhis-Bareev, Minsk 1987. The weak pawns on c6 and e6 tie Black down and leave him without counterplay.
7 g3
7 a4 c5! 8 dxc5 ♗xc5 9 e3 ♘h6 10 ♗xc4 ♘c6 11 0-0 ♘f7 is at least equal for Black.
7 ...   b5
8 ♗g2   ♘e7
It is not often that Black develops his first piece on move eight!
9 0-0?!
After 9 e4 g6 10 0-0 ♗g7 White has some compensation for the pawn. The text move allows Black to swap his superfluous knight on e7.
9 ...   ♘d5
10 b3? (D)
This allows Black to establish a strong passed pawn on c3. No better was 10 ♘e4 ♗e7 11 b3 f5! and White is in trouble, so he should have tried 10 e4! intending to set up a strong centre to compensate for the pawn, although Black can easily hold his own.
10 ...   ♘xc3
11 ♗xc3   b4
12 ♗e1   c3
13 ♕c2
After 13 a3 c5 14 dxc5 ♕xd1 15 ♖xd1 a5! Black also retains his giant protected passed pawn on c3.
13 ...   a5
14 a3   ♖a6

| 15 | Rd1 | Be7 |
| 16 | Nh4?! | c5! |

Black already has a winning position.

17	d5	Rd6
18	e4	g5!
19	e5	fxe5
20	f4	exf4
21	Nf3	Rxd5
22	Bf2	g4
23	Ne5	f3 *(D)*

Black's sixteen pawn moves have brought him total triumph! White could well have resigned here.

24 Bh1 Rd2 25 Rxd2 Wxd2 26 We4 Wd5 27 We3 Rf8 28 h3 Rf5

29 Nxg4 Bg5 30 We1 Bd2 31 Wb1 Ba6 32 Rd1 Wd3 33 Wa1 e5 34 axb4 c2 0-1

Instead of weakening the kingside with 5...f6, Black sometimes plays the queen move 5...Wc7. In the next game Ivanchuk builds up a strong centre and starts the attack with the sharply calculated central breakthrough 13 d5! Sorokin sacrifices the exchange for two pawns resulting in uncompromising fighting chess and one of the most complex Noteboom games ever played.

Game 2
Ivanchuk – Sorokin
Sochi 1986

(1 d4 d5 2 c4 e6 3 Nc3 c6 4 Nf3 dxc4 5 Bg5)

| 5 | ... | Wc7 |
| 6 | a4 | |

6 e4 b5 7 a4 Bb4 simply transposes to the game.

| 6 | ... | Bb4 |

7 e4

After 7 g3 Ne7 8 Bg2?! (8 e4 b5 leads to positions similar to the note 8 g3 at White's eighth move) 8...Nd5 9 Wc2 b5 10 0-0 Nxc3 11 bxc3 Bd6 followed by 12...Bb7 and 13...0-0 White hardly has sufficient compensation for the pawn. In general the exchange of a pair of knights helps Black.

7 ... b5
8 ♗e2

A number of other moves have been tried here, but none of them cause Black any real trouble:

- 8 ♘d2!? a6 9 axb5 cxb5 (Black plays an interesting exchange sacrifice; after 9...♗xc3 10 bxc3 cxb5 11 ♗e2 ♗b7 12 0-0 ♘e7 13 f4 0-0 White has some compensation for the pawn) 10 ♘xb5 axb5 11 ♖xa8 ♗b7 12 ♖a1 (12 ♖a7 ♕b6) 12...♗xe4 13 ♕g4 f5 14 ♕g3 ♗d6 15 ♕h3 ♗d5 16 ♗e2 ♘e7 with a balanced position in the game Bagirov-Chekhov, USSR 1982.
- 8 g3 ♘f6 (8...♘d7 followed by 9...♘gf6, or 8...a6 would have been better) 9 ♗xf6 gxf6 10 ♗g2 ♗b7 11 0-0 ♘d7 12 axb5 ♗xc3 13 bxc3 cxb5 14 d5 ♘c5 15 ♘d4 a6 16 dxe6 fxe6 17 ♕h5+ ♔e7 18 ♖fe1 and White was better in McCambridge-Strugatsky, San Mateo 1989.

8 ... ♘f6!?

This is the most ambitious setup. Black accepts some disruption of his pawn structure to get rid of White's dark-squared bishop. Preparing 9...♘gf6 with 8...♘d7 has not been tried in practice, but seems worth a try.

9 ♗xf6 gxf6
10 0-0 ♗b7

10...♗xc3!? (Black delays ...♗b7 and just develops his kingside) 11

bxc3 0-0 12 ♕c1 ♘d7 13 ♕h6 ♔h8 14 e5 ♖g8 15 exf6 ♗g6 16 ♕h5 ♘xf6 17 ♕e5 ♕xe5 18 ♘xe5 ♖g7 19 ♘xc6 bxa4 20 ♗f3 ♘d5 21 ♗xd5 exd5 and Black kept his extra pawn in the game Pushkov-Tregubov, Sochi 1993.

11 axb5 ♗xc3
12 bxc3 cxb5
13 d5! exd5

13...a6 was played in Gaprindashvili-Kilpi, Helsinki open 1992. It is hard to believe that Black can afford this move, and even more difficult to believe that Black in the end won this game after an incredible number of missed chances by the former women's world champion. There followed 14 dxe6 fxe6 15 ♘d4 ♘d7 16 ♘xe6 (better is 16 ♗h5+ ♔e7 17 ♕g4 ♕b6 18 ♕g7 with a winning initiative for White) 16...♕e5 17 ♗g4 (threatening 18 ♘g7+) 17...♖g8 18 ♖e1?! (the immediate 18 f4 is preferable, because 18...♕xe4 19 ♘c7+ ♔f8 20 ♗f3 ♕e3+ 21 ♔h1 is crushing) 18...♔e7 19 f4 ♕d6 20 ♘d4 ♕xf4 21 ♗xd7 ♔xd7 22 ♘xb5+ ♔e7 23 ♘d4 ♗xe4 (Black makes a living by grabbing everything) 24 ♕c2 (24 ♕e2! ♖g4 25 h3 ♖h4 26 ♕xc4 f5 27 ♖ab1 with a winning attack) 24...♖g4 25 ♖e2?? (25 h3! ♖h4 26 ♕e2! ♔f7 27 ♕xc4+ ♔g6 28 ♘e6 ♕e5 29 ♘c5 or 27...♖g8 28 ♘f3 f5 29 ♘xh4 ♕xh4 30 ♖xa6 in both cases with a huge plus) 25...♖xg2+ 26 ♖xg2 ♗xc2 27 ♘xc2 ♔f7 28 ♖f1 ♕e5 0-1.

14 ♘d4

14 exd5 ♕c5 15 ♖e1 0-0 16 ♕d4 ♕xd4 17 ♘xd4 a6 18 ♗f3 ♖d8 19 ♘f5 gives White good compensation in the endgame, but Ivanchuk prefers to sacrifice another pawn.

| 14 ... | a6 |
| 15 ♗h5! | |

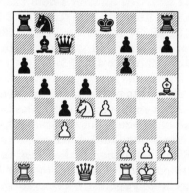

| 15 ... | dxe4 |

15...♕d7 16 exd5 ♗xd5 17 ♖e1+ is too dangerous for Black.

16 ♘e6	♕d7
17 ♕g4	♔e7
18 ♕g7	♕xe6
19 ♕xh8	*(D)*

This position is very difficult to assess. Black has three pawns for the exchange, but his h-pawn will not survive for long. With his next move Sorokin provokes a weakening of the white kingside. In the sequel of the game he misses some chances to profit from it. An alternative way is to play 19...♘d7 20 ♕xh7 f5, when Black has compensation for the exchange.

| 19 ... | ♕f5!? |
| 20 g4! | ♕e6 |

Black's queen must return to e6. After 20...♕f3 (threatening 21...e3) 21 ♕xh7 (but not 21 ♖e1 ♘d7 22 ♕xh7 ♘e5 23 g5 ♕f4 with an unclear position) 21...e3 22 ♕xf7+ ♔d6 23 ♖ad1+ ♗d5 (after king moves Black is mated very quickly) 24 ♖xd5+ ♕xd5 25 ♕xf6+ ♔c7 26 fxe3 White has a superior position.

21 f4!

White should not allow his opponent to play the manoeuvre ...♘b8-d7-e5-f3, which is possible after 21 ♕xh7 for example.

| 21 ... | ♕b6+!? |

Also good is 21...e3 22 g5 (forced to prevent 22...♕e4) 22...♘d7 23 ♕xh7 e2 24 ♗xe2 fxg5 25 fxg5 ♕e3+ 26 ♖f2 ♕xg5+ 27 ♔f1 ♘f6 28 ♕f5 ♕xf5 29 ♖xf5 ♘d5 with the better endgame for Black.

22 ♖f2	♘d7
23 ♕xh7	♖f8
24 g5	

With the horrible threat of g5-g6-g7, etc.

| 24 ... | ♘c5 |
| 25 ♗e2 | ♘d3 |

26 ♗xd3   cxd3

Black has obtained a very unusual pair of passed pawns for the Noteboom!

27 ♖e1   fxg5
28 fxg5   ♕g6?

A serious misjudgement by Sorokin. With accurate play Ivanchuk demonstrates that the resulting endgame is won for White. Black should have played 28...d2! 29 ♖f1 (or 29 ♖d1 e3 30 ♖e2 ♕c5 31 ♕h4 ♖g8 32 ♖1xd2 ♖xg5 33 ♔f1 ♗g2+ 34 ♖xg2 exd2) 29...♕e6!? 30 ♕h4 (30 ♕f5 e3 31 ♕xe6+ fxe6! 32 ♖xf8 e2 and Black wins) 30...e3 31 g6+ ♔e8 32 gxf7+ ♔d7 33 ♕d4+ ♗d5 and wins. The remaining moves need no further comment.

29 ♕xg6 fxg6 30 ♖xf8 ♔xf8 31 ♔f2 ♔e7 32 ♔e3 ♔d6 33 ♖f1 a5 34 ♖f6+ ♔c5 35 ♖xg6 a4 36 ♖f6 a3 37 h4 a2 38 ♖f1 b4 39 cxb4+ ♔xb4 40 g6 ♗d5 41 h5 ♔a3 42 h6 d2 43 h7 1-0

In the following three games we look at the kingside fianchetto by which White hopes to lure his opponent into Catalan-like positions. Black will generally keep his extra pawn on c4, but has to defend accurately against White's central and kingside attack. The next game is a good example of White's attacking chances.

Game 3
Sunye Neto – Petursson
Manila interzonal 1990

(1 c4 e6 2 ♘c3 d5 3 d4 c6 4 ♘f3 dxc4)

5 g3

With this set-up White does not even try to regain his c4 pawn, but quickly develops his kingside and follows up with e2-e4-e5 and ♘g5. Play has great similarities with the Catalan Opening, and transpositions are possible, particularly when Black plays an early ...♘f6.

5 ...   b5
6 ♗g2

6 a4 is considered in game 5. If White has not played e2-e4 then he has another plan in ♘f3-e5 with pressure on the queenside. Black should always be prepared to meet this possibility.

6 ...   ♗b7

6...♘f6 7 ♘e5 ♗b7 transposes to a variation of the Catalan that is considered good for White, as it is not easy for Black to develop his pieces. It is safer to prepare ...♘g8-f6 with 6...♘d7, to make ♘f3-e5 unattractive. This continuation is considered in game 4.

7 0-0

Or 7 e4 (7 ♘e5 f6 8 ♘f3 ♗b4 and 9...♘e7 is fine for Black) 7...♘f6 and then:

- 8 e5 ♘d5 9 ♘g5 ♘a6!? (9...♘d7 10 0-0 is the text continuation) 10 0-0 ♕d7 11 ♕h5 h6 12 a4 ♘ab4 13 ♖d1 a6 14 ♘ce4 g6 15 ♕h3 0-0-0 16 ♘f3 ♕c7 17 ♗d2 ♔b8 18 ♘e1 ♕b6 19 ♕g4 ♖d7 20 ♕f3 c5 ½-½ in Petursson-Sherbakov, Bern open 1992.
- 8 ♘e5 ♘bd7 9 f4 c5! 10 d5 b4! 11 ♘b5 a6 and Black was better in Pähtz-Lukov, Halle 1987.

7 ...   ♘d7

After 7...♘f6 8 ♘e5 ♕b6 (better is 8...♘d5) 9 a4 a6 10 e4 ♘bd7 11 ♘xd7 ♘xd7 12 d5 cxd5 13 exd5 White held the advantage in the game Shabalov-Martinov, Moscow 1987. With the game move Black first discourages 8 ♘e5.

8 e4

8 ♖b1 (8 a4 a6 will most likely transpose to game 5) was played in Rausis-Nikolov, Sofia 1989. After the continuation 8...♘gf6 9 b3 cxb3 10 ♕xb3 ♗e7 11 ♘e5 ♘d5? 12 ♘xb5 cxb5 13 ♕xb5 ♗c8 14 ♕c6 ♘b6 15 ♖xb6 axb6 16 ♕xa8 White was on top. Not much better is 10...b4 11 ♘a4 (not 11 ♘e5 bxc3 12 ♕xb7 ♖b8 and Black wins) 11...♗a6 12 ♖e1 ♗e7 13 ♗d2

♖b8 14 ♘e5 ♘xe5 15 dxe5 ♘d5 16 e4 with advantage to White, but 10...a6! 11 e4 (11 ♘e5 ♘xe5 12 dxe5 ♘d7 and 11 a4 b4 are fine for Black) 11...♗e7 followed by ...0-0 gives White only minimal compensation for the pawn.

After 8 ♘e5!? Black has to play accurately to neutralize the white pressure. The best continuation is 8...♕c7! (8...♘xe5 9 dxe5 ♕c7 10 ♘e4! ♖d8 11 ♕c2 ♕xe5 12 ♗f4 ♕f5 13 b3 leaves White with strong pressure for the pawn) 9 ♗f4 (9 ♘e4 ♘gf6! and not 9...♘xe5 10 dxe5 ♕xe5 leading to the previous note) 9...♘xe5 10 ♗xe5 (10 dxe5 ♘e7! to meet 11 ♘e4 by 11...♘d5) 10...♕d7 11 ♘e4 f6 12 ♗f4 g5! 13 ♗d2 h5!? 14 e3 h4 15 ♕f3 0-0-0 with a complex position in which Black's chances proved to be fine in Lputian-Sveshnikov, Sochi 1993.

8 ...   ♘gf6
9 e5

If White does not undertake immediate action, Black quickly develops his kingside and reaches a good position. For example 9 ♘h4 ♗e7 10 a3 0-0 11 f4 ♘b6 (but not 11...♕b6?! 12 ♗e3 c5?! 13 d5 exd5 14 exd5 ♖fe8 with a promising position for White in Tjiam-Van der Werf, Nijmegen 1993 – see the introduction) 12 ♗e3 ♕c7 intending ...a7-a6 and ...c6-c5.

9 ...   ♘d5
10 ♘g5

In this position Black has tried three different methods to defend against the threat of 11 ♕h5.

10 ...   ♗e7

The other two possibilities are:

- 10...h6 (according to our analysis the best move for Black) 11 ♕h5 g6 12 ♕h3 ♘xc3?! (better is 12...♗e7 leading to the game Sunye Neto-Petursson with an extra tempo for Black; for example 13 ♘ce4 c5 or 13 ♘ge4 b4 14 ♘a4 ♕a5 and Black is okay) 13 bxc3 ♘b6 (13...♗e7 is better, although 14 ♘xe6 fxe6 15 ♕xe6 still appears dangerous) 14 ♘xe6 fxe6 15 ♕xe6+ ♕e7 16 ♗xc6+ (an improvement is 16 ♕xg6+ ♔d7 17 f4 with good chances for White) 16...♗xc6 17 ♕xc6+ ♔f7 18 ♖b1 ♕e6 19 ♕f3+ ♔g7 20 ♖xb5 ♖d8 with a very unclear position which Black eventually won in Dunnington-Tiller, Gausdal 1987.
- The second interesting alternative, 10...♘7b6, was played in Haik-Kharlov, Metz 1993, but after 11 ♕h5 g6 12 ♕f3 ♕d7 13 a4 ♘xc3 14 bxc3 ♘d5 15 ♘e4 a5? (15...a6 16 ♗g5) 16 axb5 White seized the upper hand. Play con-

tinued 16...♗e7 17 bxc6 ♗xc6 18 ♗h6 a4 19 ♖fb1 a3 20 ♕e2 f5 21 exf6 ♘xf6 22 ♖xa3 ♖xa3 23 ♖b8+ ♕d8 24 ♖xd8+ ♔xd8 25 ♘xf6 ♗xg2 26 ♔xg2 ♗xf6 27 ♕xe6 ♗e7 28 d5 1-0.

11 ♕h5   g6?!

Better is 11...♗xg5 12 ♗xg5 ♕b6 13 ♖fe1 (or 13 ♘e4) 13...♘xc3 14 bxc3 c5 15 d5 0-0 16 ♖ad1 though White has good compensation for the pawn according to Sunye Neto.

12 ♕h6   ♗f8
13 ♕h3   ♗e7
14 ♘ce4   ♕c7?

Black should play 14...♕b6 directly, but after the continuation 15 ♘d6+ ♗xd6 16 exd6 (threatening 17 ♘xe6) 16...♗f8 17 ♖e1 (renewing the threat) 17...♗c8 18 ♕h6 ♖g8 (18...♗d7 19 ♕g7) 19 ♘xh7 White has the advantage.

15 ♖e1   ♕b6
16 ♘d6+!   ♗xd6
17 exd6   0-0-0

Black doesn't have a better alternative. 17...♘f8 fails to 18 ♘xe6 fxe6 19 ♖xe6+ ♔d7 (19...♔f7 20 ♗xd5 cxd5 21 ♖e7+ ♔g8 22 ♕h6 also wins) 20 ♖f6+ ♔e8 (20...♔d8 21 ♗g5) 21 ♖xf8+! ♔xf8 (21...♖xf8 22 ♕e6+ wins) 22 ♗h6+ ♔f7 23 ♕d7+ ♔f6 24 ♗h3 and Black is mated on e6 or g7.

18 ♘xf7   ♕xd4
19 ♕xe6! (D)

Black has no way to avoid loss of the exchange, so White can afford to wait until move 23 before taking one of the rooks.

19 ...   ♕f6

20 &h3   &xe6
21 &xe6   c5
22 &g5   &df8
23 &xh8   &xh8
24 &ae1   &c6

25 &e8+   &xe8
26 &xe8+   &b7
27 &e7   &b6
28 &xh7   b4
29 &d8

Not the most accurate move, but Black is lost in any case.

29...c3 30 bxc3 bxc3 31 &g5 &a6 32 &e7 &b5 33 &g2 &xg2 34 &xg2 &b4 35 h4 &a3 36 g4 c2 37 h5 gxh5 38 gxh5 &f6 39 &xa7+ 1-0

Clearly the quiet 5 g3 is dangerous. In the following game Black adopts a subtle move-order which turns out very well for him.

Game 4
Vasilchenko – Stripunsky
Pardubice 1995

(1 d4 d5 2 c4 c6 3 &f3 e6 4 &c3 dxc4 5 g3 b5 6 &g2)

6 ...   &d7

Black prepares ...&g8-f6. The delay of ...&c8-b7 has some subtleties that favour Black.

7 0-0

7 &e5 is dubious, due to 7...&xe5 8 dxe5 &xd1+ 9 &xd1 &b7! 10 &xb5 0-0-0+ 11 &d6+ &xd6 12 exd6 &xd6+ 13 &c2 &e7.

7 ...   &gf6

7...&b7 transposes to the previous game. The advantage of playing 7...&gf6 is that the system 8 e4 followed by the advance e4-e5 and &g5 with dangerous attacking chances is much weaker than in game 3. Moreover it anticipates &f3-e5, as after exchanging on e5 the knight can go to the ideal d5 square.

8 &g5

Alternatives are:
- 8 e4 &e7! (8...&b7 is game 3, Black should avoid 8...b4 9 &a4 &xe4 10 &e5 &xe5 11 &xe4 &d7 12 &xc6 &b8 13 &f4) 9 e5 &d5 10 &e4 (by comparison with game 3, here 10 &g5 is not possible) 10...h6 followed by ...0-0 and ...c6-c5 with equality.
- 8 &e5 &xe5 9 dxe5 &xd1 10 &xd1 &d5 is equal.
- 8 &g5 &d5 9 e4 &xc3 10 bxc3 &e7 (but not 10...h6? 11 &xe6!)

11 h4 ♘f6 12 e5 ♘d5 13 ♘e4 0-0 14 h5 h6 15 g4 Lputian-Kaidanov, Washington 1994 and now Kaidanov's proposal 15...♖b8 16 f4 f5 17 exf6 ♘xf6 18 ♘xf6+ ♗xf6 19 ♗xc6 b4 looks promising for Black.

8 ... ♗b7
9 a4 a6

Less effective is 9...b4 10 ♘e4 ♗e7 11 ♗xf6 gxf6 (or 11...♘xf6 12 ♘e5) 12 ♕c1! ♗a6 13 ♕h6 ♕a5 14 ♕g7 ♖f8 15 ♕xh7 0-0-0 16 ♖fc1 and White held the advantage in Sosonko-I.Sokolov, Dutch championship, Amsterdam 1995.

10 ♘e5 ♕c8!

After 10...♘xe5 11 dxe5 ♕xd1 12 ♖fxd1 ♘d5 13 axb5 axb5 14 ♖xa8 ♗xa8 15 e4 Black has some problems.

11 ♘xd7 ♘xd7
12 e4 b4
13 ♘b1 a5
14 ♘d2

The aggressive 14 d5 poses no problems after 14...e5.

14 ... ♗a6

15 ♖e1 c3
16 bxc3 bxc3
17 ♘b1 ♗b4

Although White will finally regain his pawn, Black has smoothly developed his pieces and now uses the time it takes White to capture on c3 to start activities in the centre and on the queenside.

18 ♕c2 e5
19 ♗e3

This looks rather strange but after 19 dxe5 ♘xe5 20 ♘xc3 0-0 21 ♖ed1 ♕g4 22 ♗e3 ♘f3+ Black has the initiative.

19 ... 0-0
20 ♘xc3 ♖e8
21 ♖ec1?!

Now Black moves in with his knight. White should have prevented this with 21 ♗h3, leading to an unclear position.

21 ... ♘b6
22 dxe5 ♘c4
23 ♗f4 ♕e6
24 ♘d1?

In order to play ♘d1-e3 to swap Black's outpost on c4, but this is too slow. It is better to occupy the f1-a6 diagonal with 24 ♗f1.

24 ... ♗a3
25 ♖cb1 ♗c5
26 ♘b2 ♗d4!
27 ♘xc4 ♗xc4

Of course not 27...♗xa1 28 ♘d6 and White has no more problems.

28 ♖a3 ♖ab8
29 ♗f1 ♗xf1
30 ♔xf1 ♖b4!

Now Black threatens to invade the white position with 31...♖eb8 and 32...♖b2. White prevents this but he is in for a nasty surprise.

31 ♗d2?   ♕h3+
32 ♔g1   ♗xf2+! *(D)*

The battle has now switched to the kingside.

33 ♔h1

33 ♔xf2 ♕xh2+ 34 ♔f3 ♖xb1 35 ♕xb1 ♕xd2 and Black wins.

33 ...   ♖xb1+
34 ♕xb1   ♕g4
35 ♔g2

35 ♗xa5 was more resilient, although Black retains the initiative after 35...♕e2 36 ♕d3 ♕b2 37 ♗d2 ♕xe5.

35...   ♗d4
36 ♖f3   ♗xe5

The rest of the game is a matter of technique. The remaining moves were:

37 ♕b3 ♖e7 38 ♕d3 ♖d7 39 ♕c2 ♗c7 40 h3 ♕e6 41 ♖c3 h5 42 ♗e1 ♖d6 43 ♖c5 ♕h6 44 ♕e2 ♖d4 45 ♖xh5 ♕e6 46 ♗xa5 ♖xa4 47 ♗d2 ♖a2 48 ♔f3 ♕d7 0-1

In the next game White tries an earlier a2-a4 but he can hardly hope for an advantage with this plan.

Game 5
B. Martin – Antunes
Manila olympiad 1992

(1 d4 d5 2 c4 e6 3 ♘c3 c6 4 ♘f3 dxc4 5 g3 b5)

6 a4

This is the most accurate move order for White in the g3 system with a2-a4, since after 5 a4 ♗b4 6 g3 Black has the interesting possibility 6...c5!? which is analysed in game 8.

6 ...   ♗b4
7 ♗g2   ♗b7
8 0-0   a6
9 e4

9 ♘e5 f6 and now:
- 10 f4 (a dubious piece sacrifice) 10...fxe5 11 fxe5 ♘d7 12 axb5 axb5 13 ♖xa8 ♗xa8 14 ♗h3 ♘f8 15 e4 ♘e7 16 ♗e3 ♘eg6 and White didn't have enough compensation in the game Hajek-Mitura, Luhačovice 1993.
- 10 ♘f3 ♘e7 11 ♗h3 ♗xc3 (alternatively 11...♕d7!?) 12 bxc3 ♗c8 13 ♗a3 0-0 14 ♕c2 ♖e8 15 e4 e5 16 ♗xc8 ♘xc8 17 ♖fd1 ♕c7 18 ♖d2 ♘d7 19 ♖ad1 and in

the game Garcia Ilundain-Anguix Garrido, Ibercaja open 1993, White's pressure along the d-file provided compensation for the pawn.

9 ...   ♘f6 (D)

9...h6!? was played in Arzhenkov-Abrosimov, Kstovo open 1994. After 10 axb5 axb5 11 ♖xa8 ♗xa8 12 ♘e5 ♘f6 13 f4 ♘bd7 14 ♘xd7 ♕xd7 15 e5 ♘d5 16 ♘xd5 (better is 16 ♘e4 although it allows Black to play 16...c3, after which 17 bxc3 ♘xc3 18 ♘xc3 ♗xc3 19 ♗e3 0-0 is fine for Black) 16...cxd5 17 ♕c2 0-0 18 f5 exf5 19 ♖xf5 ♕e6 20 g4 (but not 20 ♗h3? g6 21 ♖h5 ♕b6 22 ♖xh6 ♕xd4+ and ...♕xe5) 20...f6! 21 ♗h3? (21 ♗f4) 21...fxe5 22 ♖xe5 ♕xe5! 23 dxe5 ♗c5+ 24 ♔g2 d4+ 25 ♔g3 d3 26 ♕d2 ♖f3+ 27 ♔h4 ♗f2+ 0-1.

10 ♕c2

10 e5 ♘d5 11 ♘e4 ♘d7 (11...h6!) 12 ♗d2 ♗f8? (12...♗e7) 13 ♘fg5 ♗e7 14 ♕h5 g6 15 ♕h6 ♗f8 16 ♕h3 ♗e7 17 ♖fe1 and White was clearly better in Murshed-Flear, Calcutta open 1991.

10 ...	♗e7
11 ♖d1	0-0
12 axb5	axb5
13 ♖xa8	♗xa8
14 ♗g5	h6
15 ♗xf6?!	

It is certainly not desirable for White to give up his bishop pair, but Black has already solved his opening problems.

| 15 ... | ♗xf6 |

16 d5	cxd5
17 exd5	exd5
18 ♘xd5	♗xd5
19 ♘e1	♘c6!

Black brings out his last piece and retains his extra pawn.

20 ♖xd5	♕e7
21 ♖d1	♘d4
22 ♕d2	♖d8
23 ♔f1	b4

With an extra pawn and active pieces, Black is already winning.

24 ♕e3	♕c7
25 ♗e4	♗g5!
26 f4	♗f6
27 ♗b1	g6
28 ♖d2	♔g7
29 ♕e4	♘b3!

This is the correct moment to swap rooks. After the exchange White is no longer able to prevent all of Black's threats: 31...♘d2+, 31...♗xb2, 31...♕d1 and 31...♕d2.

The game ended:

30 ♖xd8 ♕xd8 31 ♕c2 ♕d5 32 ♔f2 ♘d2 33 ♕d1 ♗d4+ 34 ♔e2 ♕e6+! 35 ♗e4 ♕xe4+ 36 ♔xd2 c3+ 0-1

2 White avoids the main line after 5 a4 ♗b4

After 1 d4 d5 2 c4 e6 3 ♘c3 c6 4 ♘f3 dxc4 5 a4 ♗b4 most games transpose to the main variation after 6 e3 b5 7 ♗d2. This chapter only deals with attempts by White to avoid the main line. In game 6 White plays 6 e4 in order to occupy the centre immediately. The solid continuation 6 ♗d2 is the subject of game 7 and 8, and in game 9 White plays a kingside fianchetto with 6 g3 and 7 ♗g2.

Game 6
Theulings – Kroeze
Dutch championship
semi-finals, Enschede 1994

(1 ♘f3 d5 2 d4 c6 3 c4 dxc4 4 a4 e6 5 ♘c3 ♗b4)

6 e4

The actual move order in the game was 6 ♗d2 a5 7 e4 b5.

6 ... b5

7 ♗d2

7 ♗e2 (7 ♗g5 ♕c7 transposes to game 2 and 7 g3 ♗b7 8 ♗g2 a6 9 0-0 to game 5) 7...♗b7 8 0-0 a6 and now:

- 9 ♕c2 ♘f6 10 ♗g5 ♕b6 11 e5 ♘d5 12 ♘e4 ♘d7 13 ♗d2 ♗e7 14 ♗g5 ♗f8 15 b3 h6 16 ♗d2 cxb3 17 ♕xb3 ♗e7 18 ♗d3 0-0 19 ♘g3 ♖fc8 and Black did not have any problems in Najdorf-Larsen, Havana olympiad 1966.
- 9 ♗g5 ♗e7 10 h4 h6 11 ♗xe7 ♘xe7 12 ♕d2 ♘d7 13 ♖fd1 0-0 14 ♕f4 ♘f6 15 ♘e5 ♕b8 16 ♕e3 ♖d8 17 f4 ♕c7 18 ♗f3 ♘d7 with

balanced chances, Lputian-Wolff, Tilburg (rapid) 1992.

7 ... a5

7...♗b7 8 axb5 ♗xc3

- 9 ♗xc3 cxb5 10 b3 a5 transposes to the game.
- 9 bxc3 cxb5 10 ♕b1!? (10 ♘e5 ♘bd7 11 ♕b1 a6 12 ♘xd7 ♕xd7 13 f3 ♗b7 was equal in Murdzia-Gdanski, Gdansk 1994) 10...♗c6 11 ♘e5 a6 12 ♗e2 ♘e7 13 ♗c1 0-0 14 ♗a3 and White had some compensation in Dzhandzhava-Gofstein, USSR 1987.

8 axb5

White aims for the main line of the Noteboom variation with his e-pawn on e4 instead of e3. This line is not particularly dangerous, but Black has to be aware of some finesses.

8 ... ♗xc3

9 &xc3

9 bxc3 cxb5 10 &b1 &d7 11 &c2 &f6 12 e5 &d5 13 &g5 was unclear in Haik-Barle, Athens 1971.

9 ...   cxb5

10 b3

10 &e2 &f6 11 &c2 &b7 is very good for Black.

10 ...   &b7

Even stronger is 10...&f6! 11 &b1 &b7 12 bxc4 &xe4 13 &xb5+ &c6 14 &b2 &xc3 15 &xc3 &xf3 16 &xf3 (16 gxf3 does not lose a pawn, but it looks awful) 16...&xd4 and Black was simply a pawn up in the game Foisor-Dolmatov, Groningen 1977.

11 d5!?

White should not play in similar fashion to the main line with 11 bxc4, as after 11...b4 12 &b1 (otherwise White loses a pawn) 12...f5! 13 &d3 (13 exf5 &xf3 and White loses a piece) 13...&f6 Black has the better position.

11 ...   &f6

12 bxc4   &xe4!? *(D)*

12...b4 13 &xf6 &xf6 14 e5 &f4 15 &a4+ &d7 16 &d1 is dangerous for Black and 12...exd5 13 cxd5 0-0 14 &xf6 &xf6 15 &xb5 &a6 16 0-0 &c5 17 &e2 &g6 18 &fe1 is also good for White.

13 &xg7   &g8

14 &d4   exd5

15 cxb5   &e7!?

This practically forces White's next move, after which Black wins the pawn on g2. Safer is 15...&d7 with the idea of ...&c5-e6.

16 &e2   f6

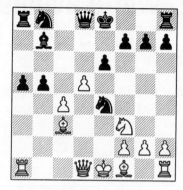

17 &h6   &xg2

18 &h4!   &xf2!?

Black decides to sacrifice the exchange for two pawns, as 18...&g8 19 &f5 holds no appeal.

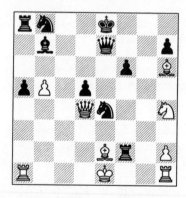

19 &e3!   &xe2+

After 19...&g8 20 &f5 the black position is a wreck.

20 &xe2   &d7!?

21 &ab1   &g4+

22 &f3   &c6!?

23 bxc6   &a6+

24 &d1

After 24 &e1 &xf3 White has no defence against the threats of 25...&e2 mate and 25...&xh1+.

24 ...　　♕xf3+
25 ♔c2　　♖c8?

The critical line runs 25...♕g2+
26 ♗d2 (forced) 26...♖c8! 27 ♖be1
♖xc6+ 28 ♔b1 ♗c4, when Black
has three pawns for the exchange
and an ongoing initiative. The
text move allows the White king to
escape to the fairly safe corner a1.

26 ♔b2　　♕g2+
27 ♔a1　　♗c4
28 ♕b2　　♕xb2+
29 ♔xb2　　♖xc6

In the resulting endgame Black
has three pawns for the exchange.
This material balance is not unfavourable, but all his pawns are
weak.

30 ♖a1　　♖a6
31 ♖hg1　　♔f7
32 ♖g4　　♘d6
33 ♗c5　　♘b5
34 ♖e1　　♖e6
35 ♖xe6　　♔xe6
36 ♖g7　　d4
37 ♖xh7　　f5 *(D)*
38 ♗xd4!

With this neat little combination White wins another pawn,

and the resulting endgame is easily won. Here are the remaining
moves:

38...♘xd4 39 ♔c3 ♔e5 40 ♔xc4
f4 41 ♔d3 a4 42 ♖a7 ♘b3 43
♔e2 ♔f5 44 ♖xa4 ♔g4 45 ♖c4
♘a5 46 ♖c5 ♘b3 47 ♖d5 ♘c1+ 48
♔d2 ♘b3+ 49 ♔c2 f3 50 ♔xb3
f2 51 ♖d1 ♔h3 52 ♖f1 ♔g2 53
♖xf2+ ♔xf2 54 h4 1-0

By playing 6 ♗d2 White post-
pones his choice between e2-e3
and e2-e4. In game 7 Black tries to
take advantage of this delay by
transposing to a kind of Queen's
Gambit Accepted.

Game 7
Lobron – I. Sokolov
Biel interzonal 1993

(1 ♘f3 d5 2 d4 c6 3 c4 dxc4 4 a4
e6 5 ♘c3)

Sokolov is an expert on the system 5 e3 b5 6 axb5 cxb5 7 b3 ♗b4+.
Hence Lobron allows a transposition to the Noteboom variation.

5 ...　　♗b4
6 ♗d2

With this useful waiting move
White protects the knight before
he decides whether to play e2-e3
or e2-e4. A typical idea in this

variation is that White sometimes prepares e2-e4 with ♕d1-b1.

6 ... ♘f6

The safest method for Black to reach a good position. The alternatives are 6...a5, which we analyse in game 6, and 6...b5 7 axb5 ♗xc3 8 ♗xc3 cxb5 9 d5 (9 e3 transposes to the main line) 9...♘f6 10 d6!? 0-0 11 ♘e5 a5 12 ♕d4 ♗b7 13 ♘g4 ♘bd7 with equal chances in Minnis-Gudmundsson, Buenos Aires olympiad 1939.

7 e3 0-0

Black can also play ...c6-c5 immediately, for example 7...c5 8 ♗xc4 ♘c6 (8...cxd4 9 ♘xd4 gives White a small plus) 9 dxc5 ♗xc5 10 0-0 0-0 11 ♕e2 e5! 12 ♘g5 ♗f5 13 ♖ad1 ♕e7 14 f3! (14 ♕f3 ♗c2 15 ♖c1 ♗g6 16 ♘ge4 ♘xe4 17 ♘xe4 ♗b4 is worse) 14...♗g6? (14...♖ad8 15 ♘ge4 ♘xe4 16 fxe4 ♗e6 17 ♘d5 ♕h4 is unclear) 15 ♘ge4 ♘xe4 16 ♘xe4 ♗b4?! (after 16...♗xe4 17 fxe4 White gets a strong light-squared bishop and control of the d5 square, which provides more than enough compensation for his ugly doubled e-pawn. Black's best move is 16...♗b6, after which White is slightly better) 17 ♗d5! ♔h8 (safer is 17...♖fd8) 18 ♕b5 ♖ab8! (18...f5? fails to 19 ♗xc6 ♗xd2 20 ♖xd2 bxc6 21 ♕c5) 19 ♗xb4 (19 ♗xc6 bxc6 20 ♕xc6 ♖fc8 21 ♕a6 ♗xe4 22 fxe4 ♖c2 23 ♗xb4 ♕xb4 is fine for Black) 19...♘xb4 20 ♕c5? (correct is 20 ♗b3! ♗xe4 21 fxe4 ♘c6 with the advantage) 20...♕xc5 21 ♘xc5 ♗c2! 22 ♖d2 ♖bd8 23 e4

b6 24 ♘a6 ♘xd5 25 exd5 ♗xa4 26 ♖a1 ♗d7 ½-½ (Hertneck-Kasparov, Baden-Baden 1992).

The natural 7...b5 is a mistake, because Black can no longer play the thematic ...a7-a5 and ...b5-b4 without making concessions, due to the pin on the a-file. For example 8 axb5 ♗xc3 9 ♗xc3 cxb5 10 b3 a5 11 bxc4 ♘e4 (it is hardly ever good in the Noteboom to occupy e4 with either bishop or knight, as White can easily chase it away or exchange it under favourable circumstances) 12 ♗b2 b4 13 ♗d3 f5 14 ♗xe4 fxe4 15 ♘d2 and Black's position was horribly weakened in Hertneck-Kaiser, Bundesliga 1990.

8 ♗xc4 ♘bd7
9 0-0 c5
10 ♕e2

10 ♕b3 b6 11 d5 exd5 12 ♗xd5 ♘xd5 13 ♕xd5 gives White a small plus.

10 ... b6
11 ♖fd1 ♗b7

Sokolov plays a Queen's Gambit Accepted in which White has played the less useful 5 a4 and 6 ♗d2.

12 ♖ac1 ♕e7
13 ♗a6 ♗xa6
14 ♕xa6 e5! *(D)*

With this strong advance in the centre Black seizes the initiative. His immediate threat is 15...e4.

15 dxc5

Both 15 d5 e4 and 15 dxe5 ♘xe5 16 ♘xe5 ♕xe5 are fine for Black.

15 ... ♘xc5
16 ♕c4 a5

17 e4   ♖ac8
18 ♘b5
The alternatives are:
- 18 ♗g5? ♘xa4! 19 ♘d5 ♖xc4 20 ♘xe7+ ♗xe7 21 ♖xc4 ♘xb2 and Black wins.
- 18 ♘d5 ♘xd5 19 exd5 ♗xd2 20 ♘xd2 (20 ♖xd2 e4 21 ♘d4 ♕d7 22 ♖dc2 ♖fe8 threatening both 22...♖e5 and 22...e3 also gives Black a slight plus) 20...♕d7 21 b3 ♖fd8 22 ♘e4 (better is 22 ♘f3, although Black still has a slight advantage) 22...♘b7! 23 ♕d3 ♖xc1 24 ♖xc1 ♕xd5 and the position is very good for Black.

18 ...   ♗xd2
19 ♘xd2   ♖cd8!
By unpinning his knight on c5, Black threatens 20...♘d3.

20 ♕e2!
A fine temporary pawn sacrifice.

20 ...   ♘xa4
Black accepts the offer. Afterwards the players concluded that 20...♘d3 21 ♖b1 ♘f4 was much better. Both 22 ♕f1 ♕b4! and 22 ♕e1 ♘g4! are very good for Black.

21 ♘c4   ♖xd1+
22 ♖xd1   ♕b4?!
22...♕c5 immediately was preferable.

23 ♘bd6   ♕c5
23...b5? 24 ♘xe5 ♘xb2 25 ♘c6 ♕b3 allows the nice queen sacrifice 26 ♕c2! After 26...♕xc2 27 ♘e7+ ♔h8 28 ♘xf7+ ♖xf7 29 ♖d8+ Black is mated.

24 g4!?	**h6**
25 h4	**♕c7**
26 ♘xe5	**♘c5**
27 ♕c4	**b5**
28 ♕xb5	**♘cxe4**
29 ♘xe4	**♘xe4**
30 ♕d5	**♕c2**
31 ♖f1	**a4**
32 h5?	

White could have defended himself better with 32 f3 ♘f6 33 ♕d4 followed by 34 ♖f2.

32 ...	**♘g5**
33 f4?	**♘h3+**
34 ♔h1	**♘xf4!**
35 ♕f3	**♘e6**
36 ♘xf7	**♕c7**
37 ♕e4	**♘g5?**

Here 37...♘d8! was easily winning.

38 ♘xh6+?

In time-trouble both players overlooked 38 ♘xg5! ♖xf1+ 39 ♔g2 hxg5 40 ♔xf1 ♕c1+ 41 ♔g2 ♕xb2+ 42 ♔h1 ♕b5 43 ♕e6+ and the game should end in a draw. White saw nothing better than sacrificing a piece, but the resulting endgame is hopeless. The remaining moves were:

38...gxh6 39 ♕g6+ ♕g7 40 ♖xf8+ ♔xf8 41 ♕d6+ ♔g8 42 ♕d5+ ♕f7 43 ♕d8+ ♔g7 44 ♕d4+ ♕f6 45 ♕d7+ ♘f7 46 ♕xa4 ♕xb2 47 ♕d7 ♕f2 48 ♕e6

♕f6 49 ♕d7 ♕d6 50 ♕f5 ♘g5 51 ♕c8 ♕e6 52 ♕c3+ ♔f7!

The easiest way to win is to walk the king into the enemy position.

53 ♕c7+ ♔e8 54 ♕b8+ ♔d7 55 ♕a7+ ♔c6 56 ♕a4+ ♔d5 57 ♕d1+ ♔e4 58 ♕f1 ♕d5 59 ♔h2 ♕a2+ 0-1

An alternative answer to 6 ♗d2 is 6...a5, inviting White to transpose to the main variation with 7 e3. In game 8 White played Hertneck's interesting idea, 7 ♕b1!?, to prevent ...b7-b5 and prepare e2-e4.

Game 8
Urban – Van der Vorm
Kiekrz team tournament 1995

(1 d4 d5 2 ♘f3 c6 3 c4 e6 4 ♘c3 dxc4 5 a4 ♗b4 6 ♗d2)

6 ...   a5

This move leads to more complicated play than the safe 6...♘f6.

7 ♕b1

Preventing 7...b5 and preparing 8 e4. After 7 e3 b5 play transposes to the main line, and 7 e4 b5 8 axb5 ♗xc3 9 ♗xc3 cxb5 is game 6.

7 ...   ♘d7

8 e4

Or 8 e3 ♘b6 9 ♘e5 ♘f6 10 ♘xc4 ♘xc4 11 ♗xc4 0-0 12 0-0 e5 with equality.

8 ...   ♘b6

9 ♗e2   f5!?

Fighting for the e4 square. After the quieter continuation 9...♘f6 10 0-0 0-0 11 ♗g5 ♗e7 12 ♖d1 White has a small but lasting advantage.

10 exf5

10 0-0 ♘f6 11 ♗g5?! (11 exf5 transposes to the game) 11...h6 12 ♗xf6 ♕xf6 13 ♕a2 0-0 14 ♗xc4 ♘xc4 15 ♕xc4 ♗d7 16 ♘e5 ♗e8 17 exf5 ♕xf5 was Hertneck-Backwinkel, Bundesliga 1987. Black has a fine position.

10 ... exf5
11 0-0 ♘f6
12 ♕a2

After 12 ♖e1 0-0 13 ♕a2 ♗e6 14 ♘g5 ♗f7 15 ♘xf7 ♖xf7 16 ♗xc4 ♘xc4 17 ♕xc4 ♕d7 similar positions arise to the game.

12 ... ♗e6
13 ♘g5 ♗g8
14 ♖fe1 ♗e7

14...♔f8 15 ♗f1 h6 16 ♘f3 followed by ♘e5 is fine for White.

15 ♗f1

After 15 ♖ad1 Black has a solid continuation in 15...h6 16 ♘f3 ♗f7 17 ♘e5 0-0, although the pin on the a2-g8 diagonal makes his task a little more difficult than in the game.

15 ... h6!

The alternatives 15...♕d7 16 ♕a3! h6 (16...♘e4 17 ♘cxe4! and 16...♔f8 17 ♕a2!) 17 ♖xe7+ ♕xe7 18 ♖e1 ♕xe1 19 ♗xe1 hxg5 20 ♕c5, and 15...♕d6 16 g3! h6 17 ♗f4 ♕d7 18 ♘f3 followed by ♘e5 are excellent for White. In the game Black voluntarily invites the white knight to e6.

16 ♘e6

After 16 ♘f3 ♗f7 17 ♘e5 0-0 Black also has no problems.

16 ... ♗xe6
17 ♖xe6 0-0
18 ♗xc4 ♘xc4
19 ♕xc4 ♔h8
20 ♖ae1

Black can meet 20 ♕d3?! with 20...♗c5, and after 20 ♘e2?! ♘d5 Black had a nice position in Hertneck-R.Kuijf, Tilburg 1994. The best move is however 20 ♗f4! which secures White a tiny plus after 20...♕d7 21 ♖ae1. After the text move Black immediately takes control of the b8-h2 diagonal and reaches an equal position.

20 ... ♗d6

½-½

In the next game White plays a kingside fianchetto with the inclusion of 5 a4 ♗b4. Black has the option of switching to game 5, which is perfectly playable for him, or, alternatively he can continue ...c6-c5 as Bagirov does in the following game.

Game 9
Steinbacher – Bagirov
Berlin open 1993

(1 d4 d5 2 c4 e6 3 ♘c3 c6 4 ♘f3 dxc4 5 a4 ♗b4)

6 g3	**c5!?**

Just as in game 7, it is possible to profit from an early a2-a4 by changing plans to the advance of the c-pawn. Black has a number of alternatives:

- 6...b5 leads to game 5.
- 6...a5 was played in Seirawan-Korchnoi, Bad Kissingen 1981. After 7 ♘e5 ♘f6 8 ♗g2 ♘d5 9 ♗d2 ♘b6 10 e3 ♘8d7 11 f4 0-0 12 ♘e4? (12 ♕e2) 12...f6 13 ♘xd7 ♕xd7 14 0-0 ♘d5 Black was a little better.
- 6...♘f6 7 ♗g2 0-0 8 0-0 ♘bd7 9 ♕c2 ♕e7 10 ♗f4 ♘d5 11 ♗d2 a5 12 e4 ♘5b6 13 ♗e3?! (13 e5 f5 14 exf6 ♘xf6 15 ♖e1 was preferable) 13...h6?! (after 13...f6 14 e5 ♘d5 Black has no problems) 14 ♖ad1?! e5 15 dxe5 ♗c5?! 16 ♗f4 ♖e8 with roughly equal chances in the game Gelfand-Anand, Moscow 1992.

7 ♗g2

After 7 ♗e3 ♘f6 8 dxc5 ♘d5 9 ♕d4 ♘xe3 10 ♕xe3 ♕c7 11 ♕e5 ♕xe5 12 ♘xe5 ♘d7 13 ♘xc4 ♘xc5 14 ♗g2 ♔e7 15 0-0 ♗xc3 16 bxc3 ♗d7 Black had a slight plus in the game Roobol-R.Kuijf, Netherlands 1994.

7 ...	**♘c6**
8 ♗e3	**♘f6**
9 0-0	**♘g4**
10 ♘e5?!	

10 ♘e4 was played in Ragozin-Tal, Riga 1951. After the continuation 10...0-0 11 ♖c1 cxd4 12 ♗xd4 f5 13 ♘eg5 h6 14 ♘h3 e5 15 ♗c3 ♗d6 16 ♕d5+ ♔h7 17 ♕xc4 ♕e7 18 e4 f4 Black had a good position. The text move, however, is not an improvement.

10 ...	**♘cxe5**
11 dxe5	**♘xe3**
12 ♕xd8+	**♔xd8**

| 13 | fxe3 | ♔e7 |

The resulting ending is fine for Black. For the time being he has an extra pawn and after his next move he can smoothly complete the development of his pieces.

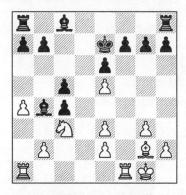

| 14 | ♖f4 | ♗d7! |
| 15 | ♗xb7 | |

After 15 ♖af1 ♖hf8 White is practically forced to take on b7 anyway.

15	...	♖ab8
16	♗a6	♗a5
17	♗b5	♗c8!

Black prepares ...a7-a6.

18	♖af1	♖f8
19	♘e4	♗c7
20	♘d6!?	

This is the most practical move. If White allows ...a7-a6 Black gains a strong initiative straight away.

20	...	♗xd6
21	exd6+	♔xd6
22	♖xf7	♖xf7
23	♖xf7	a6
24	♗xc4	♖xb2
25	♖xg7	♖b4
26	♗d3	h6!

In order to make two passed pawns on the kingside, White would now have to manoeuvre his rook to h6, where it is awfully located to stop the black passed c-pawn.

| 27 | a5 | c4! |

White has no chance against Black's strong passed pawn.

28 ♗g6 c3 29 ♖g8 ♗d7 30 ♖a8 ♗b5 31 ♖c8 ♖c4 32 ♖xc4 ♗xc4 33 ♔f2 ♔c5 34 ♔e1 ♔b4 35 ♔d1 ♔xa5 36 ♔c2 ♔b4 37 ♗e8 ♗b3+ 38 ♔c1 a5 39 ♔b1 a4 40 ♗g6 a3 41 g4 a2+ 42 ♔a1 ♔a3 43 h4 c2 44 ♗xc2 ♗xc2 0-1

3 White does not play 7 ♗d2

After the standard moves 1 d4 d5 2 c4 e6 3 ♘c3 c6 4 ♘f3 dxc4 5 a4 ♗b4 6 e3 b5, White has a number of alternatives to 7 ♗d2. The best and most popular of these options is 7 ♘d2, a move that strenghtens White's control over e4 and makes way for the queen to attack on the kingside. The next game shows how such a strategy can be successful.

Game 10
Beliavsky – Kharlov
Soviet team championship 1991

(1 d4 d5 2 c4 e6 3 ♘c3 c6 4 ♘f3 dxc4)

5 a4

This move order is more forcing than 5 e3 b5 6 a4, when Black can try 6...b4!? instead of the standard move 6...♗b4. Play might continue 7 ♘e4 (or 7 ♘a2 ♗a6 and White can hardly regain his pawn) 7...♗a6 8 ♕c2 ♕d5 9 ♘ed2 c3 10 bxc3 bxc3 11 ♕xc3 ♗xf1 12 ♘xf1 a5 with equality.

5 ...	♗b4
6 e3	b5
7 ♘d2	♕b6

7...♕d7 is considered in the next game.

Sveshnikov, who is a Semi-Slav expert, played 7...♗b7 in his game with Delemarre in Tilburg 1994. After 8 ♕f3 a6 9 ♕g3 ♘f6 10 ♗e2 0-0 11 0-0 ♘bd7 12 ♗f3 ♕b8 he was simply a pawn up. In Kiselev-Dgebuadze, Pardubice 1995, White tried 8 ♕g4, but Black won in attractive style after 8...♘f6! 9 ♕xg7

♖g8 10 ♕h6 a6 11 ♕h3 c5 12 dxc5 ♘bd7 13 e4 ♘xc5 14 ♗e2 ♘cxe4 15 ♘dxe4 ♘xe4 16 ♕xh7 ♖xg2 17 ♕h8+ ♔d7 18 ♕d4+ ♔e7 19 ♗e3 ♕xd4 20 ♗xd4 ♖d8 21 ♗f3 ♘xc3 22 ♗xb7 ♘xa4+ 23 ♔e2 ♖gg8 24 ♗e3 a5 25 ♗c6 ♘xb2 26 ♗xb5 c3 27 h4 ♖b8 28 ♗a6 ♖bd8 0-1. White should have played 8 axb5 ♗xc3 9 bxc3 cxb5 10 ♖b1 ♗c6 11 ♕g4 with excellent compensation.

8 ♕g4

In Van Wely-Nogueiras, Matananzas 1994, White had sufficient compensation after 8 ♕f3 ♗b7 9 ♕g3 ♔f8 10 ♗e2 ♘f6 11 0-0 a6 12 ♘de4 ♘bd7 13 ♘d6.

8 ... ♔f8

Black tried 8...g6 to preserve the right to castle in the game Tisdall-Wikström, Hallsberg 1996, but when he finally did castle it did not bring him much joy: 9 ♕g3 ♘d7 10 ♗e2 ♘gf6 11 h4 ♗b7 12 0-0 a6 13 ♘de4 ♘xe4 14 ♘xe4 0-0-0?! 15 ♗d2! ♗xd2 16 ♘d6+ ♔b8 17

♘xc4+ ♕c7 18 ♕xc7+ ♔xc7 19 ♘xd2 and White had a solid positional advantage.

9 g3

9 ♗e2 ♘f6 10 ♕g3 ♗b7 leads to Van Wely-Nogueiras. After 9 axb5 cxb5 10 ♘d5 exd5 11 ♕xc8+ ♔e7 12 g3 ♕c6 Black was better in Iljinsky-Sherbakov, Novgorod 1995.

9 ...	♘f6
10 ♕f3	♗b7
11 ♗g2	a6
12 0-0	♘bd7

13 axb5

Another plan is to build a kingside attack with 13 g4, followed by ♕g3 and h2-h4. In Speelman-Flear, London 1986, White chose to become active on the other side with 13 ♘a2 ♗d6 14 b3 cxb3 15 ♘xb3, but should have been worse after 15...♖b8 with the intention of ...c6-c5. Beliavsky decides to attack through the centre.

13 ...	axb5
14 ♖xa8+	♗xa8
15 ♘de4	♔e7
16 ♘xf6	♘xf6

17 e4   c5?

Now Black is in real danger. He should have captured a second pawn, though White has some attacking chances after 17...♕xd4 18 ♖d1 ♕c5 19 g4!

18 d5!

Usually ...c6-c5 is not a good move if White can reply with d4-d5. Here this breakthrough is possible as both 18...exd5 19 ♘xd5+ ♗xd5 20 exd5 and 18...♗xc3 19 ♕xc3 exd5 20 ♕e5+ ♕e6 21 ♕c7+ ♘d7 22 exd5 ♗xd5 23 ♗xd5 ♕xd5 24 ♖e1+ give White a powerful initiative.

18 ...	♖e8
19 ♗g5	e5
20 ♗xf6+	gxf6
21 ♘d1	

More straightforward is 21 ♘e2 followed by g2-g4, ♘g3 and ♘f5. Now Black prevents 22 ♘e3.

21 ...	♗d2
22 ♕e2	♕a5
23 f4	exf4
24 gxf4	c3
25 bxc3	♗xc3

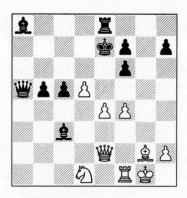

26 ♘xc3?!
26 e5 would have been more aggressive, putting the black king in all sorts of trouble. Beliavsky takes a pawn in order to restore the material balance.

26 ...	♕xc3
27 ♕xb5	♕d4+
28 ♔h1	♔f8
29 ♕a6	c4
30 ♖g1	♔g7
31 ♕b5	♖d8
32 ♕a5	♖f8
33 ♕a3	♖e8
34 ♕d6	c3?

This is the decisive mistake. Better was 34...♔h8 with chances for both sides.

35 e5

35 ...	fxe5

Equally unpleasant is 35...♕xf4 36 exf6+ ♕xf6 37 ♗f3+.

36 ♗e4+	♕xg1+
37 ♔xg1	exf4
38 ♕xf4	h6
39 ♕g3+	♔f8
40 ♕xc3	1-0

White has enjoyed some success with 7 ♘d2, but the next game shows a new strategy for Black, which is based on controlling the e4 square with a pawn on f5. This positional theme is quite common to the Noteboom variation.

Game 11
Delemarre – Van der Werf
Wijk aan Zee 1995

(1 d4 d5 2 c4 e6 3 ♘f3 c6 4 ♘c3 dxc4 5 a4 ♗b4 6 e3 b5 7 ♘d2)
7 ...   ♕d7!
At first sight this move looks rather strange, but it is perfectly

logical. The idea is to play ...f7-f5 in order to gain control over the important e4 square. The queen will defend the pawns on b5 and g7. White's knight has just gone to d2, but after ...f7-f5 its best square is e5.

8 ♕f3   ♗b7
9 ♕g3   f5!

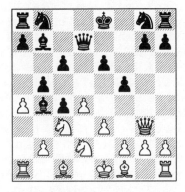

10 axb5

White has two alternatives. The sharp continuation 10 e4 ♘f6 11 exf5 0-0 12 fxe6 ♖e8 leaves the white king in trouble, while after the quiet 10 ♗e2 ♘f6 11 0-0 0-0 12 e4 a6 13 exf5 exf5 Black is better since 14 ♘f3 ♗xc3 15 bxc3 ♘e4 favours Black.

10 ...   ♗xc3

This is forced, since 10...cxb5 11 ♘xb5 ♕xb5 12 ♕xg7 is disastrous.

11 bxc3   cxb5
12 ♗a3

With this move White prevents castling, but Black can get his king to safety anyway.

12 ...   ♘f6
13 ♗e2   ♘c6
14 ♗c5?!

Now White's compensation vanishes. Better is 14 0-0 and 15 ♖fb1 at once, although Black's chances are slightly better.

14 ...   ♔f7
15 0-0   ♖hc8

Where to put the rook? This eternal question has two plausible answers – on e8 where it prepares the counterblow ...e6-e5, or on c8 as in the game where it indirectly looks at the bishop on c5. The text move works out well, but both ideas seem equally strong.

16 ♖fb1   a6
17 ♗f3   ♔g8

Black has finally completed his development. He now tries to exchange pieces and carry forward his extra pawn into the endgame.

18 ♖a2   ♘d8
19 ♗d1   ♘e4
20 ♘xe4   ♗xe4
21 ♗c2   ♗xc2
22 ♖xc2   ♘b7
23 ♗a3   ♕c7
24 ♕f3   ♕c6
25 e4?

White hopes to create counterplay, which he would achieve after 25...♕xe4 26 ♕xe4 fxe4 27 ♖e2. However, 25 ♕f4 is better.

25 ...   fxe4
26 ♕g4   ♖e8?

Much better was the immediate 26...e5!, after which Black keeps the e4 pawn with a decisive advantage. In the game White keeps some initiative although it is not enough to save the game.

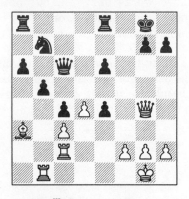

27 ♖e2   e5
28 ♖xe4   exd4
29 ♖xd4   ♕e6
30 ♕xe6+   ♖xe6

Black has finally reached his goal: he is a pawn up in the endgame. Despite this White still has some drawing chances, but in the game Black's extra pawn proved to be enough to win, but only after a long struggle.

31 ♖d7 ♘a5 32 g3 ♘c6 33 ♖bd1 ♘e5 34 ♖d8+ ♖e8 35 ♖xe8+ ♖xe8 36 ♖d6 ♖a8 37 ♗c5 ♖c8 38 ♗e3 ♖c6 39 ♖d8+ ♔f7 40 ♔g2 ♘g4 41 ♗d4 ♘f6 42 ♖b8 ♖d6 43 ♔f3 g6 44 h4 h5 45 ♖b7+ ♔e6 46 Bxf6 ♔xf6 47 ♔e4 ♖e6+ 48 ♔f4 ♖d6 49 ♔e4 ♖d3 50 ♖b6+ ♔f7 51 ♖xa6 ♖xc3 52 ♖b6 ♖b3 53 ♔e5 b4 54 ♖b7+ ♔e8 55 ♔e6 ♔f8 56 ♖f7+ ♔g8 57 ♖c7 c3 58 ♖c8+ ♔g7 59 ♖c7+ ♔h6 60 ♖c4 ♖b2 61 f4 c2 62 f5 gxf5 63 ♔f6 ♖a2 64 ♖c8 ♖a6+ 65 ♔f7 ♖a7+ 66 ♔f6 ♖a6+ 67 ♔f7 ♔h7 68 ♖xc2 b3 69 ♖f2 ♖b6 70 ♖b2 ♔h6 71 ♔e7 ♔g6 72 ♔d7 f4 73 gxf4 ♔f5 74 ♔c7 ♖b4 75 ♔c6 ♔xf4 76 ♔c5 ♖b8 77 ♔d4 ♔g4 78 ♔e4 ♔xh4 79 ♔f4 ♖b4+ 80 ♔f3 ♔g5 81 ♔g3 h4+ 82 ♔f3 ♔f5 83 ♔e3 ♔g4 84 ♖g2+ ♔h3 85 ♖b2 ♔g3 86 ♖b1 b2 0-1

The final game of this chapter shows a different plan for White: quick development followed by a kingside attack. Black proves to have a very solid position; his defence looks very natural and his win is convincing, demonstrating the perfect Black strategy.

Game 12
Dive – Tregubov
Groningen open 1994

(1 d4 d5 2 c4 c6 3 ♘f3 e6 4 ♘c3 dxc4 5 a4 ♗b4 6 e3 b5)
      7 ♘e5

In the game Bangiev-Varga, Budapest 1989, White had some compensation after 7 ♗e2 ♗b7 8 0-0 a6 9 ♘a2 ♗d6 10 b3 cxb3 11 ♕xb3 ♘e7 12 ♗a3. In fact he even won this game, but that was not because of the opening. Black's position would have been ideal after 9...♗e7 followed by ...♘f6 and ...0-0.

7 ...   ♘f6

In Delcroix-Kharlov, Torcy open 1991, Black played a strong sequence of moves which brought him an advantage: 7...♕e7!? 8 ♗d2 ♘f6 9 axb5 ♗xc3 10 ♗xc3 cxb5 11 ♗a5 ♘fd7! 12 b3 (12 ♕f3? ♘xe5 13 ♕xa8 ♘ec6, followed by trapping the queen by means of ...♗b7) 12...♘xe5 13 dxe5 ♘c6.

8 ♗e2   ♗b7
9 0-0   a6
10 f4

White has to do something, otherwise Black will consolidate his position and retain the extra pawn.

10 ...   0-0
11 ♗f3   ♘d5!

Now White would like to play 12 ♘e4, but this loses a knight after 12...f6 13 ♘g4 f5.

12 ♗d2   ♗e7
13 ♗e4

Better was 13 e4 ♘b4 14 ♗e3 although the strong centre is not sufficient compensation for the pawn. In the game White's attack with g2-g4 and g4-g5 is harmless, because Black hits the centre with ...c6-c5.

13 ...   g6
14 g4   ♘d7
15 g5   c5!

Unlike Beliavsky-Kharlov, here this advance secures a huge advantage for Black.

16 ♕f3   cxd4
17 exd4   ♘xe5
18 dxe5   ♖b8
19 axb5   axb5
20 ♖fd1   ♕b6+

Black would also have played this move after 20 ♔g2. His plan is quite simple: push the queenside majority.

21 ♔g2   ♖fd8
22 ♘e2   ♗b4
23 ♔g3   ♗xd2
24 ♖xd2   ♖d7
25 ♖ad1   b4
26 h4   ♖bd8
27 h5   c3

Starting the decisive attack.

28 bxc3   bxc3
29 ♖c2   ♘xf4!
30 ♖xd7   ♘xh5+
31 ♕xh5   gxh5
32 ♖xb7   ♕e3+
33 ♗f3   ♖d3

0-1

4 First move-order dilemma

After 1 d4 d5 2 c4 e6 3 ♘c3 c6 4 ♘f3 dxc4 5 a4 ♗b4 6 e3 b5 7 ♗d2 Black has several possibilities. He can move his queen to e7 or b6, as considered in game 13, but in our opinion Black does better to play either 7...a5 or 7...♗b7. Normally these continuations lead to the main variation which has the typical move order 8 axb5 ♗xc3 9 ♗xc3 cxb5 10 b3. However there are some differences, which we will discuss in this chapter and the initial games of the following chapter:

7 ...   a5
- allows 8 ♘e5 (game 14)
- makes it necessary to defend the pawn on b5 with a piece instead of a pawn after 8 ♖b1 and 8 axb5 ♗xc3 9 bxc3 (games 15 and 17)
- virtually stops 10 d5 (game 19)

7 ...   ♗b7
- allows 8 b3 (game 16)
- anticipates 8 ♘e5 (game 16)
- discourages 8 axb5 ♗xc3 9 bxc3, since Black can easily protect the pawn on b5 with ...a7-a6.
- allows 10 d5 although Black can obtain a small edge (game 18)

The choice between 7...a5 and 7...♗b7 is a matter of taste, but we start our discussion with the less common 7...♕e7 and 7...♕b6. Although a clear-cut refutation has not yet been found, the conventional moves, 7...a5 and 7...♗b7, are more trustworthy.

Game 13
Schneider – Z. Varga
Budapest 1989

(1 d4 d5 2 c4 c6 3 ♘c3 e6 4 ♘f3 dxc4 5 a4 ♗b4 6 e3 b5 7 ♗d2)
7 ...   ♕e7

This variation was popular for a while, but after some impressive White victories Noteboom players have turned back to conventional moves. A rare but interesting alternative is 7...♕b6 which led to equality in Lautier-Granda Zuniga, Biel interzonal 1993, after 8 axb5 cxb5 9 ♘e5 ♗b7 10 b3 ♘c6! 11 bxc4 ♗xc3 12 ♗xc3 ♘xe5 13 dxe5 bxc4 14 ♖b1 ♕c6 15 ♖b4 ♗a6 16 ♗e2 ♘e7 17 ♗f3 ♘d5 18 ♗xd5 exd5 19 0-0 ♗c8 20 ♕d4 0-0. It looks rather unnecessary for White to exchange immediately on b5.

The alternative 8 ♘e4 yielded White compensation in the game Spasov-Popov, Bulgaria 1985, after 8...♗e7 (but not 8...♗xd2+ 9 ♘fxd2

♘d7 10 ♕g4 and Black has problems) 9 b3!? cxb3 10 ♕xb3 bxa4 11 ♕xa4. The second alternative 8 ♘e5 gave White a slight advantage after 8...♘f6 (8...♘d7 9 axb5 ♘xe5 10 dxe5 cxb5 11 ♘e4 ♗e7 12 ♕g4 was better for White in Alekhine-Kashdan and Steiner, 1929) 9 axb5 cxb5 10 b3 0-0 11 bxc4 bxc4 in the correspondence game Bernitt-Standler, 1981, and now White should have played 12 ♗xc4 instead of 12 ♘xc4 ♕d8! 13 ♕f3 ♗xc3 14 ♗xc3 ♕d5 with an equal position.

A dubious alternative is 7...♘f6. After the plausible 8 axb5 ♗xc3 9 ♗xc3 cxb5 10 b3 0-0 (10...♘e4?! does not save the pawn on c4 after 11 ♗a5) 11 bxc4 bxc4 12 ♗xc4 ♕c7 13 ♕b3 a fundamental position has arisen. White has a better pawn structure, while Black has an a-pawn that may be strong and may be weak. In this case White's bishop pair gives him the better chances. In Piket-Kupreichik, Lvov 1988, the bishops soon achieved decisive strength: 13...a5 14 0-0 ♗b7 15 ♖fc1 ♘g4? 16 d5!

8 axb5   ♗xc3
9 ♗xc3   cxb5
10 d5   ♘f6
11 dxe6

Another promising continuation is 11 d6, which gave White the initiative after 11...♕b7 12 b3 0-0 13 ♗xf6 gxf6 14 ♕d4 e5 15 ♕h4 ♔g7 16 bxc4 bxc4 17 ♗xc4 ♕b4 18 ♘d2 ♕xd6 19 0-0 in M.Gurevich-Kaidanov, Lvov 1987. Black played

the natural 12...cxb3 13 ♕xb3 a6 14 ♗xf6 gxf6 in Lesiege-Koliada, Hamilton 1994, which continued with 15 ♗e2 e5 16 ♕b4 ♗e6 17 ♕h4 ♘d7 18 ♘e5?! ♕c8! 19 0-0 ♘xe5 20 ♕xf6 ♘g6 21 f4 0-0 22 f5 ♕c5 and Black had enough counterplay. However, the simple 18 0-0 would have given White a very pleasant position, since 18...0-0? 19 ♗d3 f5 20 ♘g5 ♘f6 21 ♕h6 is forbidden. Note how useful the d6 pawn is.

11 ...   fxe6

That a draw can be spectacular is proved by the game Schmitt-Z.Varga, Altensteig 1993: 11...♗xe6 12 ♘d4 0-0 13 ♕f3 ♘d5 14 ♘f5 ♕g5 15 ♘xg7 ♘xc3 16 ♘xe6 fxe6 17 ♕xa8 ♘a6 18 f4 ♕c5 19 ♕f3 ♕b4 20 ♕g4+ ♔h8 21 ♖xa6 ♘e4+ 22 ♔e2 ♕xb2+ 23 ♔f3 ♘d2+ 24 ♔f2 ♘e4++ 25 ♔f3 ♘d2+ 26 ♔f2 ♘e4++ ½-½. *ECO* suggests 14 ♕g3 instead of 14 ♘f5 and claims an advantage for White. However, Black is simply a pawn up after the continuation 14...♘xc3 15 bxc3 a6 as 16 ♘xb5 fails to 16...♕b7 followed by ...♕b2.

12 ♘d4   0-0
13 ♘xb5   ♘e4
14 ♗xc4! *(D)*

This wild position was reached in several games. It turns out that White's chances are somewhat better.

14 ...   ♕h4

No better is 14...♘xf2? 15 ♕d6 ♕xd6 16 ♘xd6 ♗d7 (or 16...♘xh1 17 ♘xc8 ♘c6 18 ♗xe6+ ♔h8 19

②d6 and White is winning) 17 0-0
②g4 18 ②f5 ᴫf7 19 h3 ②f6 20 ②xg7
and Black's kingside was demol-
ished in Jasnikowski-Matlak, Po-
land 1988.

15 g3   ②xg3
16 ♕d4!

The boring continuation is 16
fxg3 ♕xc4 17 ♕d4 ♕xd4 18 ♗xd4
②c6 19 ♗c3 ᴫb8 ½-½ (Csonkics-
Z.Varga, Budapest 1989).

16 ...   ♕xd4
17 ②xd4   ②xh1
18 ②xe6   ♗xe6

Other continuations also lead
to defeat:

- 18...♗b7 19 ②c7+ ♔h8 20 ②xa8
  ②c6 21 ②c7.
- 18...ᴫxf2 19 ②c7+ ♔h8 20 ②xa8
  followed by 0-0-0.
- 18...②c6 19 ②xf8+ ♔xf8 20 ♗d5
  ♗b7 21 ♗xh1.
- 18...②d7 19 ②xf8+ ♔xf8 20 ♗d5
  ᴫb8 21 ♗xh1.

19 ♗xe6+   ♔h8
20 ♗d5   ②xf2

After 20...②d7 21 ♗xa8 ᴫxa8 22
f3 Black cannot save the knight.
In the game an instructive ending
arises. The bishops outclass the
knights in this very open position.

21 ♗xa8   a6
22 ♔e2   ②g4
23 h3   ②f6
24 ♗b7   ᴫf7
25 ♗f3   h6
26 ᴫa4!

The rook searches for an active
position and finds it within a few
moves.

26 ...   ♔h7
27 ᴫb4   ②bd7
28 ᴫb7   ♔g6
29 ♗d4   ᴫe7

30	♗c6	♔f7
31	♗a4	g5
32	♖a7	

Total domination!

32	...	♘b8
33	♗b3+	♔e8
34	♖a8	1-0

Black resigned as he loses material after the continuation 34...♖b7 35 ♗xf6 ♖xb3 36 ♗e5 or 34...♘d7 35 ♗a7.

Now we turn to the more conventional move 7...a5. In addition to 8 axb5, White has several ways to play for an advantage. These deviations are perfectly sound, but none of them lead to a convincing edge. The first features 8 ♘e5 which has been played in several games. White tries to exploit the f3-a8 diagonal. If Black parries the threats White tries to build a kingside attack supported by a strong centre. In game 14 White succeeds, but we shall see that Black's position is sufficiently resourceful.

Game 14
Pähtz – Flear
Bad Mondorf open 1991

(1 d4 d5 2 c4 e6 3 ♘c3 c6 4 ♘f3 dxc4 5 e3 b5 6 a4 ♗b4 7 ♗d2)

7	...	a5
8	♘e5	♘f6 (D)

In Chepukaitis-Yuneev, Leningrad 1980, White had a pleasant initiative after 8...♗b7 9 axb5 ♗xc3 10 bxc3 cxb5 11 ♖b1 ♕d5 12 ♕g4 ♔f8 13 e4 ♕xe4 14 ♕xe4 ♗xe4 15 ♖xb5 ♘f6 16 ♘xc4.

9 ♕f3

White can also play in the style of the main variation with 9 axb5 ♗xc3 10 ♗xc3 cxb5 11 b3 ♗b7 12 bxc4 b4 13 ♗b2 0-0. This position is favourable for Black due to the pressure on g2. White now played 14 ♕a4+ ♘fd7 15 c5 0-0 16 ♘xd7 in the game Piket-Kuijf, Hilversum 1986. According to Soltis Black should now have played 16...♕xd7

instead of 16...♗c6, when he secures an endgame advantage after 17 ♕xd7 ♘xd7 18 ♗b5 ♘b8!

9	...	♗xc3
10	bxc3	

Capturing with the bishop, 10 ♗xc3, is an interesting alternative. White has a slight advantage after 10...♕d5 11 axb5 cxb5 12 ♖xa5

Ξxa5 13 ♗xa5 ♕xf3?! 14 gxf3 since he controls e4 and can disrupt the black queenside with b2-b3. Black should play 13...♗b7.

10	...	♕d5
11	♕g3	0-0
12	f3	♘e8
13	e4	♕d8
14	♗e2	

Soltis gives 14 Ξb1 as a natural alternative, but the normal continuation 14...♗a6 15 ♗e2 f6 16 ♘g4 ♘d7 leads to the game. The diagrammed position is very interesting. Black has kept his pawn, but still has some work to do. The massive pawn centre and attacking possibilities give White substantial compensation.

14	...	f6
15	♘g4	♘d7
16	Ξb1	

16 0-0 ♘b6 17 f4 ♘xa4 18 ♕h4 ♗d7 is too slow. White has some play, but Black should be able to neutralize his kingside attack. In the game Panczyk-Vilela, Polonica Zdroj 1982, Black had a solid plus

after 19 f5 exf5 20 exf5 ♘d6 21 ♘e3 ♘b6. A better attempt for White is 17 Ξfb1 ♘xa4 18 ♗xc4 ♘xc3 19 ♗xc3 bxc4, as in the game Karason-Van der Werf, Reykjavik 1996 Now White should have played 20 Ξa4 instead of 20 Ξb8 Ξxb8 21 ♕xb8 ♘c7!

16	...	♗a6
17	♘e3	♔h8?

This mysterious move throws away the advantage. Better was 17...♘b6.

18	♕h3	♕e7
19	0-0	♘d6
20	♗d1	♘b6?

Black should either have played this one move earlier, or he should have played the critical 20...♘f7.

21	e5!	fxe5
22	♗c2	♘f5
23	♘xf5	exf5
24	Ξbe1!	

White does not fancy the exchange, as Black has nice compensation after 24 ♗xf5 Ξxf5 25 ♕xf5 exd4. Instead he wins the important e-pawn.

24 ...	g6
25 ♖xe5	♕d7

Other queen moves are no better. After 25...♕f7 White wins in similar fashion to the game: 26 ♗h6 ♖fe8 27 g4 f4 28 ♗xf4! ♕xf4 29 ♗xg6. And after 25...♕d6 26 ♖fe1 White invades on the e-file.

26 ♗h6	♖fe8
27 g4! *(D)*	

This blow gives White's attack decisive strength, since 27...fxg4 28 fxg4 ♖xe5 29 dxe5 ♘d5 allows 30 ♗xg6! hxg6 31 e6 ♕xe6 32 ♗e3+ ♔g8 33 ♗d4.

27 ...	♘d5
28 gxf5	♘xc3
29 ♕h4	g5

Black's position also collapses after 29...♘e2+ 30 ♔h1 ♘xd4 31 ♖xe8+ ♖xe8 32 ♕f6+ ♔g8 33 fxg6.

30 ♗xg5	♖g8
31 ♔h1	♘d5
32 ♖xd5!	cxd5

33 ♗f6+	♖g7
34 ♖g1	♖g8
35 ♖g3	1-0

Black's only 'defence' 35...♕e8 fails to 36 ♕xh7+ ♔xh7 37 ♖h3+ and mate.

In the next game White plays the unusual move 8 ♖b1, which is not without poison because of the threat of 9 axb5 ♗xc3 10 bxc3 cxb5 11 ♖xb5. Black defends well and equalizes.

Game 15
Moskalenko – Malishauskas
Norilsk 1987

(1 d4 d5 2 c4 c6 3 ♘f3 e6 4 ♘c3 dxc4 5 a4 ♗b4 6 e3 b5 7 ♗d2 a5) 8 ♖b1

White has some interesting options here. Uhlmann-Serrer, Germany 1991, featured 8 ♕b1, when instead of 8...♗d7 Black should have played 8...♗a6. In the game Lesiege-Flear, Hyères open 1992, Black quickly got into trouble after

9 ♘e4 ♘d7 10 axb5 cxb5 11 ♗xb4 axb4 12 ♘d6+ ♔e7 13 ♘e5! ♘xe5 14 dxe5. On the ninth move 9...f5 with the idea of 10 ♘eg5 ♗xd2+ 11 ♔xd2 ♕e7 is not an improvement. After 10 ♗xb4! fxe4 11 ♕xe4 axb4 12 axb5 ♗b7 13 ♖xa8 ♗xa8 14 ♕xe6+ ♘e7 15 ♗xc4 White's attack and pawns more than outweigh the knight. A better way to

keep the knight from c5 is 9...♕e7, for instance 10 ♗xb4 ♕xb4+ 11 ♘fd2 ♘d7 or 10 b3? f5.

Another serious alternative is 8 ♕c2, as played in Djurhuus-Volzhin, Oakham 1992. Black chose a normal set-up and was awarded with an edge after 8...♘f6 9 ♘e5 0-0 10 ♗e2 ♗b7 11 0-0 ♕b6 12 f4 ♘bd7.

| 8 | ... | ♗a6 |
| 9 | ♘e5 | ♖a7 |

10 ♘xc6!?

Better than the normal 10 ♕f3 ♖c7. In that position White has two possibilities: 11 ♘xc6 ♘xc6 12 axb5 ♘xd4 13 exd4 ♗b7 14 ♕g3 ♘f6 with better play for Black or 11 b3? ♗xc3 12 ♗xc3 b4 13 ♗a1 c3! 14 ♗xa6 ♘xa6 15 ♘xc6 ♕d5 16 ♕xd5 (16 ♕g3? fails to 16...♖xc6 17 ♕xg7 ♕f5 followed by 18...♕f6) 16...exd5 17 ♘xa5 ♘f6 and though White is a pawn up, the position of his bishop on a1 and knight on a5 make his position painful to observe.

| 10 | ... | ♘xc6 |

11	axb5	♗b7
12	bxc6	♗xc6
13	♗xc4	♕g5
14	d5!	

This is the only move, because now 14...♕xg2 is too risky. After 15 dxc6 ♕xh1+ 16 ♗f1 White has nasty threats, such as ♘b5 and ♕g4. After the text move the position is equal.

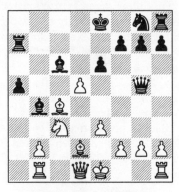

14	...	exd5
15	♗b5	♕g6
16	0-0	♘e7
17	♖c1	0-0
18	♗xc6	♕xc6
19	♘e2	♕b6
20	♘d4	a4
21	♗xb4	♕xb4
22	♖c2	♖b8
23	h4	♕d6
24	♕g4	♕d7
25	♕xd7	♖xd7

In this dead drawn position the isolated pawn does not matter. The players obviously love playing chess, however, as they continue for a few hours before they agree to an inevitable draw.

26 Ħa1 Ħa7 27 Ħd2 Ħaa8 28
h5 f6 29 Ħc2 Ħa7 30 Ħa2 Ħc8 31
Ħxc8+ ♘xc8 32 ♘b5 Ħb7 33
♘c3 ♘b6 34 Ħa3 Ħc7 35 ♘xa4
♘xa4 36 Ħxa4 Ħc1+ 37 ♔h2
Ħc2 38 Ħa8+ ♔f7 39 Ħa7+ ♔g8
40 ♔g3 Ħxb2 41 Ħd7 Ħb5 42 ♔f4
Ħb2 43 ♔f3 Ħb5 44 g4 Ħa5 45
♔g3 Ħb5 46 ♔f4 Ħb2 47 f3 Ħb5
48 g5 fxg5+ 49 ♔e5 Ħb3 50 ♔d4
h6 51 Ħxd5 ♔f7 52 Ħa5 ♔f6 53
Ħa6+ ♔f7 54 ♔e4 ♔e7 55 Ħg6
♔f7 56 Ħc6 Ħa3 57 Ħd6 Ħb3 58
f4 gxf4 59 ♔xf4 Ħb5 60 ♔g4 ½-½

The move 7...♗b7 is an important alternative to 7...a5. Usually
this leads to the main line, but in
the next game White tries to take
advantage by attacking the queenside at once. A slight edge is the
best that White can hope for. An
appealing aspect for White is that
it leads to a quiet position, since
Black usually plays the Noteboom
to create tension.

Game 16
Spraggett – Klinger
Vienna 1986

(1 d4 d5 2 c4 c6 3 ♘f3 e6 4 ♘c3
dxc4 5 a4 ♗b4 6 e3 b5 7 ♗d2)
    7 ...   ♗b7

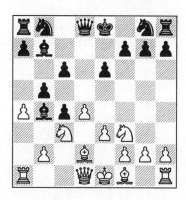

8 b3

Computer programs have also
discovered the many delights of
the Noteboom. A 486-DX2/66MHz
computer showed that 7...♗b7 anticipates 8 ♘e5 very well. In the
game P.Varga-Chess Genius, Budapest 1995, Black won convinc-
ingly: 8...♘d7 9 f4 ♘xe5 10 fxe5
♘h6 11 ♗e2 c5 12 ♗f3 ♗xf3 13
♕xf3 0-0 14 ♘xb5 ♗xd2+ 15 ♔xd2
♕b6 16 ♔c2 Ħab8 17 ♕e4 cxd4 18
♕xd4 ♕b7 19 e4 Ħfd8 20 ♘d6 ♘f5!
(a typical computer move) 21 exf5
♕xg2+ 22 ♔b1 ♕xh1+ 23 ♔a2
♕xh2 24 Ħd1 ♕c2 25 Ħg1 Ħb4 26
Ħxg7+ ♔xg7 0-1.

    8 ...   a5

Not 8...cxb3 9 ♕xb3 ♗xc3 (or
9...♕a5 10 Ħb1) 10 ♗xc3 and White
threatens both 11 axb5 and 11 d5.

    9 bxc4

9 axb5 ♗xc3 is the usual continuation, transposing to the main
line.

    9 ...   bxc4

This is better than 9...♗xc3 10
♗xc3 b4 11 ♗b2 ♘f6 12 ♗d3 c5 13

0-0 ♘bd7 14 ♖e1 and White's position plays itself (Knaak-Karasev, Polonica Zdroj 1974).

10	♗xc4	♘f6
11	0-0	0-0
12	♕e2	

12 ♘e5 c5! 13 dxc5 ♘fd7 equalized in the game Kohlweyer-Domont, Geneva 1994. Black even got the upper hand in Babula-Matlak, Moscow 1994, after some unimpressive moves from White: 12 ♖b1 ♘a6 13 ♘e2 c5 14 ♗c1 ♗e4.

12 ...   c5!

Obviously the key move in this line.

13	dxc5	♘bd7
14	c6!	

Giving up the defenceless pawn voluntarily is a well-known trick to win a tempo on the bishop.

14	...	♗xc6
15	♘d4	♗b7
16	♖fc1	♕e7
17	♗b5	♖fc8 (D)
18	♘a2?	

White should have played 18 f3 to secure a tiny advantage.

18	...	♗xd2
19	♕xd2	♘c5
20	♕e2	

Now 20 f3? is prohibited due to 20...e5 21 ♘f5 ♕e6 22 e4 ♘cxe4 (not 22...♘b3 23 ♕g5) and Black is winning.

20	...	♘d5
21	♖ab1	♕g5
22	♘f3	♕g6

22...♕f5 is more active.

| 23 | ♖b2 | ♘b4? |

Here Black should have played 23...♘e4 with equality. The text move is just a miscalculation, after which Black simply loses a pawn.

24	♘xb4	axb4
25	♖xb4 (D)	
25	...	♗d5

Black was probably counting on 25...♘d3 26 ♖xc8+ ♖xc8 but White plays the cool 27 ♗xd3 ♗xf3 (or 27...♖c1+ 28 ♕e1!) 28 ♕xf3 ♕xd3 29 h3 with excellent winning prospects. The alternative 25...♘b3 26 ♖xc8+ ♖xc8 27 h3! is not much better.

26	♘e1	h5
27	f3	♕g5

28	Rc3	Rc7
29	e4	We5
30	Rxc5!	

White has a winning position, as long as he avoids 30 Rc2 Bb3 or 30 Wc2 Rac8. Now he clarifies the position and keeps a material advantage enough to secure the point.

30	...	Rxc5
31	exd5	Wc3
32	Re4	Rxd5
33	h4	Rad8
34	Kh2	Rd4
35	f4	Rxe4
36	Wxe4	Rd4?

The position is lost anyway, but this move paves the way for a final attack.

37	Wa8+	Kh7
38	Nd3	g6
39	Wb7	Kg7
40	Be8	Rxd3
41	Wxf7+	Kh8
42	Wxg6	Wd4

1-0

Black resigned because mate or material loss is inevitable after 43 Wh6+ Kg8 44 Bg6.

5 Unusual moves in the main line

If White wishes to avoid the main line, he has a number of chances to deviate. On move 9 capturing on c3 with the pawn is an interesting alternative. The next game demonstrates the ideal strategy for Black, which is based on a tactical trick.

Game 17
Knaak – Stangl
Hamburg 1993

(1 d4 d5 2 c4 e6 3 ♘f3 c6 4 ♘c3 dxc4 5 a4 ♗b4 6 e3 b5 7 ♗d2 a5)

8	axb5	♗xc3
9	bxc3	cxb5
10	♕b1

Another plan in this position is 10 ♘e5 ♘f6 11 ♖b1 ♗a6. Matveeva-Zsu. Polgar, Moscow olympiad 1994, continued 12 ♗e2 0-0 13 f4 ♘e4 14 ♗f3 ♘xd2 15 ♕xd2 ♖a7 and Black was able to consolidate her extra pawn.

10 ... ♗d7!

It is usually best to defend the b-pawn with ...♗a6, but in this position 10...♗a6 would enable White to achieve excellent compensation after the continuation 11 ♗e2 ♘c6 12 0-0 ♘f6 13 e4. In the game M.Gurevich-Bjork, Rilton Cup 1987, Black voluntarily weakened his kingside and was severely punished: 13...h6 14 ♗d1 g5 15 ♗c1 ♕b6 16 d5 exd5 17 ♗e3 ♕c7 18 exd5 ♘xd5 19 ♕e4+ ♘ce7 20 ♗d4

with an overwhelming initiative for White.

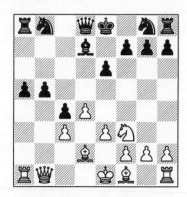

11	♘e5	♘f6
12	h4?!

An odd move that does not suit this position. After normal moves Black also carries out the plan of ...0-0 and ...♘c6, which frees his position. Here are two examples:

- 12 ♗e2 0-0 13 0-0 ♘c6 14 ♘xd7 ♕xd7 15 f4 ♖ab8 16 ♕c2 ♖fc8 17 ♗f3 b4 18 ♖fd1 bxc3 19 ♗xc3

♘d5 20 e4 ♘e3 21 ♕d2 ♘xd1 22 ♖xd1 ♕a7 and White had no compensation in Stempin-Weyrich, Copenhagen 1990.

• 12 f3 0-0 13 ♗e2 ♕c7 14 0-0 ♘c6 15 ♘xc6 ♗xc6 16 e4 e5 17 d5 ♗d7 and Black was better in Maartense-Van der Werf, The Hague 1993.

12 ...	♕c7
13 ♗e2	0-0
14 ♗f3	♘c6!

With this strong move Black secures a clear advantage.

| 15 ♘xd7 | ♕xd7 |
| 16 0-0 | |

16 ♕xb5 ♘xd4 leads to a hopeless endgame.

| 16 ... | ♖fb8 |
| 17 ♖d1 | b4! |

White has a kind of 'Benko Gambit' compensation, therefore Black pushes his pawns, even though the text move implies a pawn sacrifice. Stangl has judged the position very well and soon his knights control vital queenside squares.

| 18 ♕a2 | |

The other attempt to regain the pawn 18 cxb4 axb4 19 ♖xa8 ♖xa8 20 ♗xc6 ♕xc6 21 ♕xb4 meets with 21...♘d5 22 ♕c5? (or 22 ♕b1 c3, also with advantage for Black) 22...♕a6 (threatening 23...♖c8) 23 ♗b4 ♖c8 24 ♕d6 ♕a4 25 ♖b1 c3 and Black wins.

18 ...	b3
19 ♕a4	♘d5
20 ♖db1	♖c8
21 ♕xc4	a4!

Based on the line 22 ♖xa4? ♘e5.

22 ♕f1	♘a5
23 ♗e2	♘b6
24 ♗b5	♕b7

Again the pawn on a4 is taboo: 25 ♗xa4 ♘ac4 and White loses one of his bishops.

| 25 ♗c1 | ♘ac4 |

Although the pawn sacrifice has led to material parity, the position is not equal. White can only await his execution, which comes swiftly.

26 ♕d3	♖a5
27 ♗xc4	♘xc4
28 ♗a3	b2
29 ♗xb2	

29 ♖a2 ♕b3 is sheer masochism, but resigning is preferable in this position.

29	...	♘xb2
30	c4	♕b4
31	♕c2	a3
32	c5	h6
33	♖a2	♖b5
34	♕e2	♖cb8
35	♖ba1	♖a5
36	♕c2	♕b3
37	♕d2	♖a4
38	♔h2	♘d3

39	♕d1	♕xd1
40	♖xd1	♖b3

Now that the time-trouble is over, the game is too.

0-1

At first sight 10 d5 seems quite dangerous, but in fact Black can hold the balance. The next game shows Black's possibilities if he has played 7...♗b7, and in game 19 we present the correct answer to 10 d5 in the case of 7...a5.

Game 18
Kula – Matlak
Katowice open 1992

(1 d4 d5 2 c4 e6 3 ♘f3 c6 4 ♘c3 dxc4 5 e3 b5 6 a4 ♗b4 7 ♗d2 ♗b7)

8	axb5	♗xc3
9	♗xc3	cxb5
10	d5!?	

After 7...♗b7 this pawn advance is more viable than after 7...a5, but this game shows that even under better circumstances 10 d5 is premature.

10	...	f6

The natural developing move 10...♘f6, played in Straeter-Rausis, Hastings 1996, can hardly be recommended. White's bishops soon control the board after the continuation 11 dxe6 ♕xd1+ 12 ♖xd1 ♗xf3 (necessary because 12...fxe6 13 ♘d4 loses the extra pawn in unfavourable circumstances) 13 exf7+ ♔xf7 14 gxf3.

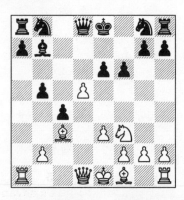

11	dxe6	♕xd1+

At first sight 11...♘c6 seems to be an improvement, because of 12 ♘d4 ♘xd4 13 ♗xd4 a6 14 ♗e2 ♘e7 or 12 ♗e2 ♘ge7 13 0-0 0-0 and Black has no problems. However, after 12 ♘d2! (threatening 13 ♕h5+) Black is in deep trouble, for example 12...b4 13 ♗xb4! ♘xb4 14 ♕h5+ g6 15 ♕b5+ or 12...a6

13 ♘e4 with the powerful threat of 14 ♘d6+.

12	♖xd1	♘e7
13	b3	

In order to generate a diversion White attacks Black's pawn chain straight away. John Nunn's suggestion of 13 ♘d4 a6 14 ♗e2 is interesting, for example 14...♘bc6 (14...0-0 15 ♗b4 and 14...♘d5 15 ♘f5 are not to be recommended) 15 ♗h5+ g6 16 ♗f3 (16 ♘xc6 ♗xc6 17 ♗xf6 ♖f8 18 ♗xe7 ♔xe7 19 ♗g4 ♖fd8 followed by ...♗d5 is equal) 16...0-0-0 17 ♘xc6 ♗xc6 18 ♗xf6 ♗xf3 19 gxf3 ♖xd1+ 20 ♔xd1 ♖e8 followed by ...♘d5 with a small plus for Black.

13	...	a5
14	♗b2	

White does not find 14 bxc4 b4 attractive and has to retreat due to the threat 14...b4 followed by ...c3.

14	...	♘bc6
15	♘d4	♘xd4
16	exd4	*(D)*

16 ♖xd4?! a4 is unpleasant for White.

16	...	♗d5

After this move Black's advantage is small. An interesting attempt is 16...a4 17 bxc4 b4 18 d5 a3 19 ♗d4 ♘f5 20 ♗c5 b3 and the situation is totally unclear. In the game Black wins the pawn on e6 but his extra pawn on c4 is too weak to offer winning chances.

17	bxc4	bxc4
18	♖c1	♖c8
19	♗a3	♗xe6

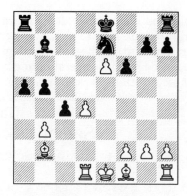

20	♗c5	♘c6
21	♗e2	

White cannot take on c4 as 21 ♗xc4 ♗xc4 22 ♖xc4 ♘xd4! leaves him a pawn down in a rook ending.

21	...	♔f7
22	0-0	♖hd8
23	♖fd1	

23 ♗xc4 ♘xd4 is Black's intention.

23	...	♖d7
24	♔f1	
24	...	♘b4

Black cannot make progress and at the same time hold on to his c-pawn, for example 24...♖cd8 25 ♗b6. The resulting position is totally drawn, and the game only lasts a few more moves.

25	♗xc4	♗xc4+
26	♖xc4	♘a6
27	♖a1	♘xc5
28	dxc5	♖a7
29	c6	♖cc7

½-½

The next two games feature a very popular line, the sharp 10 b3 and 11 d5. White takes a positional risk and Black has to defend carefully, as his king is usually stuck on the central files. A thorough knowledge and understanding of these positions is essential. Game

19 features an old line in which White eats the queenside pawns and keeps Black's king in the centre. However, Black's counter-attack is decisive.

Game 19
Serebrianik – Maksimenko
Vrnjačka Banja 1991

(1 d4 d5 2 c4 e6 3 ♘c3 c6 4 ♘f3 dxc4 5 e3 b5 6 a4 ♗b4 7 ♗d2 a5 8 axb5 ♗xc3 9 ♗xc3 cxb5)

10 b3

The immediate 10 d5 is premature since White cannot maintain a pawn on d5 after 10...♘f6. The game Donner-Pliester, Amsterdam 1982, went 11 dxe6 ♕xd1+ 12 ♔xd1 ♘e4!? 13 ♗e1 ♘c6 14 ♘d4 ♘xd4 15 exf7+ ♔xf7 16 exd4 and now 16...a4 instead of 16...♖d8 would lead to an advantage for Black. Also good is the quiet continuation 12...♗xe6 13 ♘d4 ♗d7 14 ♖xa5 ♖xa5 15 ♗xa5 ♘c6 16 ♘xc6 ♗xc6 17 f3 0-0 18 e4 ♖a8 19 ♗c3 ♖a1+ and Black's active rook and queenside majority gave him the better prospects in Kelečević-Preissmann, Switzerland 1994.

10 ...   ♗b7
11 d5   ♘f6

Here 11...f6 is impossible because of 12 bxc4 b4 13 ♗xb4 axb4 14 ♖xa8 ♗xa8 15 ♕a4+ ♘d7 16 dxe6.

12 bxc4

12 dxe6 is inconsistent and allows Black to get an active position

after 12...♕xd1+ 13 ♔xd1 fxe6 (or even 13...♘e4 14 exf7+ ♔xf7 15 ♗e1 ♖d8+) 14 ♖xa5 ♖xa5 15 ♗xa5 ♘c6 16 ♗e1 0-0 17 bxc4 b4. In the game Praszak-Trichkov, Prague 1991, Black's queenside attack was irresistible after 18 ♔c2 ♘e4 19 ♗d3 ♘c5 20 ♗e2 ♖a8.

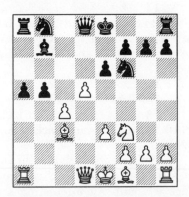

Note that the position resembles game 6 but with the white pawn on e3 instead of e4. This enables Black to push his b-pawn and avoid the tactical jungle of that game. The current game is also pretty sharp, but a Noteboom player should be able to handle that!

12 ...   b4
13 ♗xf6
White can also play 13 ♕a4+
immediately. The game Kecskes-
Weyrich, Nagykanizsa 1993, fin-
ished in a quick victory for Black
after 13...♘bd7 14 dxe6 fxe6 15
♗d4 0-0 16 ♗e2 ♕c7 17 ♖d1 ♗c6
18 ♕a1 a4 19 0-0?? ♘g4. Also possible is 13...♕d7, an invitation to
an endgame that is good for Black.

13 ...   ♕xf6
14 ♕a4+   ♘d7
15 ♘d4   e5
Very bad is 15...exd5? 16 c5, followed by c5-c6 or ♗b5. An interesting alternative is 15...♔e7, when
in the game Shulman-Petrov, Ve-
jen 1993, White played all the right
moves: 16 d6+ ♔xd6 17 ♖d1 ♔e7
18 ♘f5+ exf5 19 ♖xd7+ ♔e6 20
f3. The resulting position is not
entirely clear but Black's position
looks highly suspect.

16 ♘b3
16 ♘b5? allows 16...0-0. After
17 ♘c7 ♘c5 18 ♕b5 e4 19 ♖c1 ♕b2
Black has a crushing attack.

16 ...   ♔e7! *(D)*
The only way to parry the threat
of 17 c5.

17 ♕b5
The most principled continuation. Game 20 features 17 ♗e2
and 17 e4 is also interesting. Black
can best meet the latter move with
17...♕g6! 18 f3 ♕b6, when his control over the a7-g1 diagonal gives
him the better chances.

Also possible is 17 ♖d1 ♕b6 18
♗e2 (*ECO* suggests 18 d6+ ♔d8

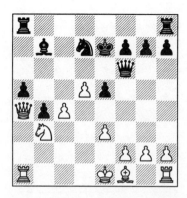

but this looks so suspicious that it
has never been tried in practice;
Black's weak bishop turns into a
powerful piece and the initiative is
with Black as he threatens ...♗c6
and ...a5-a4) 18...♖hd8 19 0-0 ♔f8
with an equal position. In Maio-
rov-Adrianov, Sochi 1980, Black
put his king on d6 and was in serious trouble after 20 c5+!

17 ...   ♗a6
18 ♕xa5   ♖hb8
19 d6+
White can try to make a draw
with 19 ♕c7 ♖c8 20 ♕a5 ♖cb8, but
he may not succeed after 20...♕d6!
threatening 21...♗xc4.

19 ...   ♔e8! *(D)*
Black cannot play 19...♕xd6, as
White has a winning position after
20 c5 ♕d5 21 ♗xa6 ♕xb3 22 0-0
♕e6 23 ♕c7! ♖xa6 24 ♖xa6 ♕xa6
25 ♖d1 (Görtz-Gonschorek, correspondence game 1988).

20 ♕d5
White also failed to prevent defeat in Ionov-Moroz, Tallinn 1984,
after 20 ♗e2 ♗b7 21 ♕c7 ♖xa1+
22 ♘xa1 ♗xg2 23 ♖g1 e4 24 ♘b3

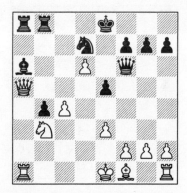

♕c3+ 25 ♘d2 ♗f3 26 ♗d1 ♗xd1
27 ♔xd1 ♖a8 28 ♘b1 ♕d3+ 29
♔c1 b3 30 ♘a3 b2+ 0-1, and in the
correspondence game Olsson-Mat-
lak, 1992, after 20 c5 ♗b7 21 ♕c7
♖xa1+ 22 ♘xa1 e4 23 ♗b5??
♕xa1+ 24 ♔d2 ♕b2+ 25 ♔d1 ♖a8
0-1.

20 ...   ♗b7
21 ♕d2
21 ♕d1 e4 22 ♖c1 ♖a2 gives
Black good prospects.

21 ...   ♖xa1+

22 ♘xa1   ♘c5
23 d7+
Or 23 ♕xb4 ♕xd6 24 ♕d2 ♕a6
and Black's initiative is killing.
23 ...   ♔d8
Normally this piece configura-
tion on the d-file indicates a winning position for White. Here,
Black wins in a few moves.
24 ♕xb4   ♕d6
25 ♕d2   ♕a6
26 ♕b2
On 26 ♕c3 or 26 ♘c2 Black decides the game with 26...♗e4.
26 ...   ♕a5+
0-1

The next game features the
same line and again it is a tactical
battle in which Black comes out
on top. Although White's 17 ♗e2
looks like a quiet move, it is actu-
ally a perilous continuation. Black
has to defend carefully but should
be able to hold the balance.

Game 20
Rogers – Krasenkov
Hastings 1993/94

(1 d4 d5 2 c4 e6 3 ♘c3 c6 4 ♘f3
dxc4 5 e3 b5 6 a4 ♗b4 7 ♗d2 a5
8 axb5 ♗xc3 9 ♗xc3 cxb5 10 b3
♗b7 11 d5 ♘f6 12 bxc4 b4 13
♗xf6 ♕xf6 14 ♕a4+ ♘d7 15 ♘d4
e5 16 ♘b3 ♔e7)
17 ♗e2 (D)
White intends 18 ♗g4 to attack
the knight on d7 in order to seize
control over the c5 square.

17 ...   ♕d6?!
This move is now considered
dubious since White has two ways
to obtain a substantial advantage.
The first way is 18 ♘xa5 as after
18...♘c5 19 ♕d1 White is simply a
pawn up and 18...♕b6 19 d6+ is
winning immediately. White's second possibility is from the instructive game Shulman-San Segundo,

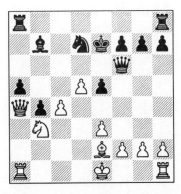

Pamplona 1995. White played 18 f4 intending to meet 18...exf4 with 19 0-0! The game went 18...♖hc8 19 0-0 ♘c5 (19...♘b6 is an interesting alternative, for example 20 ♕a2 a4 or 20 ♕b5 ♗a6. However, after 20 fxe5 ♕xe5 21 ♕b5! ♕xe3+ 22 ♔h1 ♗a6 23 d6+ ♔f8 24 ♕f5 White comes out on top) 20 ♘xc5 ♖xc5 21 ♖ad1 e4 22 ♕a1 ♔f8 23 ♕e5! ♕xe5 24 fxe5 and White won the endgame smoothly.

An interesting alternative to 17...♕d6 is 17...♕b6, completely ignoring White's ♗g4 plan. In Lacrosse-Van der Vorm, Kiekrz 1995, White first developed his kingside, but reached an inferior position: 17...♕b6 18 0-0 ♘c5 19 ♘xc5 ♕xc5 20 ♖fd1 ♖hd8 21 ♗f3 ♔f8 followed by 22...♖d6 and ...♗c8-d7. It is better for White to carry out his plan. Maurer-Mukhametov, Bern 1995, went 17...♕b6 18 ♗g4 ♘f6 19 c5 ♕a7 20 d6+ ♔f8 21 ♗f3 e4 22 ♗e2 ♗d5 23 c6 ♗xb3 24 ♕xb3 ♕c5 25 ♕c4 ♕xd6 26 c7 ♖c8 and Black was in command. Instead of 23 c6?, which drops a pawn, White should

have played 23 ♖c1 ♕d7 24 ♕xd7 ♘xd7 25 ♗b5 with a pleasant advantage.

Black's best choice, 17...♖hc8, is also the most logical one. It develops the rook and makes way for the king to go to a safer spot. White has four alternatives:

- 18 ♘xa5?! is bad on account of 18...♕b6. After 19 0-0 ♘c5 20 ♕b5 ♕xb5 21 cxb5 ♗xd5 Black has regained his pawn and has a clear advantage and 19 d6+ ♔e8 20 ♗g4 ♗c6! also looks nice for Black.

- 18 ♗g4 is critical but Black can defend with the reply 18...♕d6. After 19 ♗xd7 ♕xd7 20 ♕xd7+ ♔xd7 21 ♘xa5 (21 ♖xa5 ♖xa5 22 ♘xa5 ♗xd5 is also advantageous for Black) 21...♖c5! 22 ♘b3 ♖xa1+ 23 ♘xa1 ♖xc4 is just what Black has in mind, so in Shulman-V.Ivanov, Moscow 1995, White took a great many risks with 19 ♘xa5 ♖xa5! 20 ♕xa5 ♖a8 21 ♕xa8 ♗xa8 22 ♖xa8 ♕g6 (fortunately for Black the bishop is already on g4!) 23 ♗xd7 ♕b1+ 24 ♔e2 ♕xh1 25 ♖a7 and after both the game continuation 25...♔d6 and the alternative 25...♕c1 Black has no problems.

- 18 ♖d1 was played in Gelfand-Piket, Amsterdam 1996. After 18...♘c5?! 19 ♘xc5 ♖xc5 20 0-0 ♖a6?! (better is 20...♔f8 to get a healthy king position) 21 ♕c2 White's queen played a decisive role in a game where Black's king could not survive in the centre. Instead of 18...♘c5, Black should have delayed the exchange of knights and kept White's queen away from the centre with 18...♛d6.

- 18 0-0 has never been tested. After the continuation 18...♛d6 19 f4 we are back in the game Shulman-San Segundo. If Black wants to avoid this, Taimanov's ancient suggestion 18...♘c5 is a solid alternative, for example 19 ♘xc5 ♖xc5 20 ♖ad1 ♔f8 and now 21 ♛d7 ♗c8 does not do White any good.

18 ♗g4?   ♘b6!

A nice combination that effectively wins the game.

19 c5

Forced, since the queen moves 19 ♛a2 a4 and 19 ♛b5 ♗a6 are hopeless.

19 ...	♛xd5
20 cxb6	♗c6
21 ♛a2	♛xg2
22 ♖f1	

Or 22 0-0-0 ♛xg4 23 ♘xa5 ♖xa5 24 ♛xa5 ♛c4+ and Black wins.

22 ...	♛xg4
23 ♘xa5	♗b5

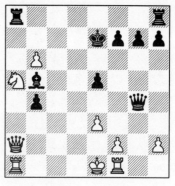

24 ♛b2	♛e4

Here the black queen controls the whole board.

25 b7	♖a6
26 ♖g1	♖d8

After 26...♖g6 27 0-0-0 the white monarch escapes, but now he cannot survive. White manages to prevent 27...♖g6, but it is to no avail.

27 ♛c1	♛d3
28 ♛b2	♔f6

0-1

The last game of this chapter features a new idea of Korchnoi's, which creates an outpost for the white knight. However, White appears to lose too much time in penetrating Black's position.

Game 21
Korchnoi – Lobron
Biel interzonal 1993

(1 d4 d5 2 c4 e6 3 ♘c3 c6 4 ♘f3 dxc4 5 a4 ♗b4 6 e3 b5 7 ♗d2 a5 8 axb5 ♗xc3 9 ♗xc3 cxb5 10 b3 ♗b7)

11 bxc4	b4
12 ♗b2	

This move is perfectly logical. The ugly 12 ♗d2 really is as bad as it looks. An example is the game Mühlenhaus-Van der Werf, Berlin open 1993, where Black had a fantastic position after 12 ♗d2 ♘f6 13 ♗d3 ♘bd7 14 0-0 ♕c7 15 ♖e1 0-0 16 e4 e5 17 ♗g5 exd4 18 ♗xf6 ♘xf6 19 e5 ♗xf3 20 ♕xf3 ♘d7.

12 ...   ♘f6
13 c5

13 ♗e2, as played in the game Belikov-Kharlov, Kuibishev 1990, is too slow. After 13...♘bd7 14 0-0 0-0 15 ♘d2 ♕c7 16 ♕c2 a4 17 ♖fb1 ♖fb8 18 h3 ♗c6 Black had the initiative. With 13 c5 White intends to create an 'octopus' on b6 or d6, but Lobron is right not to be impressed.

13 ...   0-0
14 ♘e5   ♕c7
15 ♕a4   ♖d8
16 ♖c1?!

White should have played 16 f3 to prepare for further development. Now Black finds a neat manoeuvre to seize the advantage in the centre.

16 ...   ♘c6
17 ♘c4   ♘e7
18 ♘b6

If White plays 18 f3 immediately Black can take the initiative with 18...♗c6 19 ♕b3 ♘fd5 followed by ...a5-a4.

18 ...   ♖a7
19 f3   ♘fd5!

White was prepared for 19...♗c6. After 20 ♗b5 ♘fd5 21 e4 he has counter-chances. Instead Black removes the knight which spent so much time becoming an octopus.

20 ♘xd5   exd5!

21 c6

This pawn sacrifice is forced, as 21 ♗b5 ♗c6 22 0-0 ♖b8 23 ♗xc6 ♕xc6 24 ♕xc6 ♘xc6 25 e4 ♖d7 gives Black the upper hand in the endgame.

21 ...   ♗xc6
22 ♗b5   ♖d6
23 0-0   ♕d7
24 ♖c5   ♗xb5
25 ♖xb5

The black position is also rosy without queens. After 25 ♕xb5 ♕xb5 26 ♖xb5 f5 Black moves his king to the e6 square.

25 ...   f5
26 ♖a1   ♘c6
27 ♖c5   ♕e6?

Lobron has played perfectly until this point, but now he allows Korchnoi back into the game. The best move was 27...h6 28 ♗c1 and only then 28...♕e6.

28 e4!

Black must take on e4, because 28...♖a6 is strongly answered by 29 ♕b5. Taking with the d-pawn is

not really an option, because of 29
d5, so the f-pawn does the job.

28   ...   fxe4
29   fxe4   Rf7

Again a difficult choice for Black
because capturing the e-pawn was
impossible: 29...dxe4 30 d5 Rxd5
31 Rxc6 or 29...Wxe4 30 Rxc6. Now
White can equalize with 30 e5 Wf5
31 Wc2 Wxc2 32 Rxc2 Re6 33 Rc5
Ra7. Instead a chain of mistakes
begins.

30   h3?   Wf6?

30...dxe4 was the way to embar-
rass White, e.g.: 31 d5 Wf5 32 Kh2
Nd8 33 Rxa5 Wf4+ 34 Kh1 e3.

31   Wc2?!

Here again Korchnoi misses the
possibility to equalize. This time
31 exd5 was the way to reach that
goal.

31   ...   Nxd4?

Oh no! Black could have reached
a respectable position with 31...b3
32 We2 We6 33 e5 Rd8. Now he is
in trouble.

32   Rc8+   Rf8
33   Rxf8+   Kxf8
34   Wd3??

White has a tremendous advantage after 34 Wc8+ Kf7 35 Wc7+
Ke8 36 Re1.

34   ...   dxe4
35   Wxe4   Kg8

Now Black is again in control,
as 36 Rxa5 fails to 36...Nf3+ 37
Wxf3 Wxf3 38 gxf3 Rd1+ 39 Kf2
Rb2+ 40 Ke3 Rxb2 and the rook
ending is winning.

36   Rc1   Rd8
37   Rd1   Nf3+
38   Wxf3   Rxd1+
39   Wxd1   Wxb2
40   Wd5+   Kf8
41   Wd8+   Kf7
42   Wd7+   Kf6
43   Wd6+   Kf7
44   Wd7+   Kf6
45   Wd8+

Both players realised that 45
Wd6+ Kf5! is not a repetition of
moves.

45   ...   Ke6
46   Wb6+   Kd5
47   Wxa5+   Kc4
48   Wa6+   Kc3
               0-1

A plausible continuation is 49
Wc6+ Kd2 50 Wd5+ Kc1 51 Wg5+
Kb1 52 Wf5+ Wc2, but White had
seen enough.

So these continuations should
not frighten Black at all. In the rest
of the book we shall see if the main
line is more promising for White.

6 Second move-order dilemma

This chapter deals with various possibilities on the fourteenth and fifteenth moves for both White and Black. Normally White plays 0-0 and ♕c2 in some order and Black copies these moves in some order (...0-0 and ...♕c7), taking the game into the main line which we shall discuss in chapters 7 and 8.

The next two games have some factors that are also common to the main line. The key element is that Black counters e3-e4 with ...e6-e5. If somehow this move is impossible then Black will suffer for the rest of the game. In our examples, however, Black plays instructively.

Game 22
W. Schmidt – Matlak
Polish championship, Czestochowa 1993

(1 ♘f3 d5 2 d4 c6 3 c4 e6 4 ♘c3 dxc4 5 a4 ♗b4 6 e3 b5 7 ♗d2 a5 8 axb5 ♗xc3 9 ♗xc3 cxb5 10 b3 ♗b7 11 bxc4 b4 12 ♗b2 ♘f6)

13 ♗d3   ♘bd7

In the game Knaak-Vera, Berlin 1982, Black played the unfortunate move 13...♗e4 and was struggling after 14 ♗xe4 ♘xe4 15 ♕c2 ♘f6 16 e4. The problem is that 15...f5? is impossible on account of 16 d5.

14 ♕c2   ♕c7

More straightforward is 14...0-0 15 e4 e5 and now 16 dxe5 ♘c5 is exactly what Black hopes for in the Noteboom.

15 e4   e5
16 dxe5   ♘h5 (D)

And not 16...♘g4 because of the reply 17 e6!

17 g3?

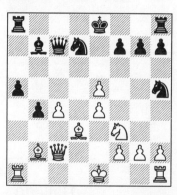

Beim-Sherbakov, Leeuwarden open 1994, continued 17 ♕d2! ♘c5 18 ♗c2 (it is nice to have some space) 18...0-0 19 g4 ♖fd8 20 ♘d4 (20 ♕e3? b3 21 ♗b1 ♕d7) 20...♘f4 and the players agreed to a draw. That is a pity, because possible continuations are spectacular, for example 21 ♕xf4 ♖xd4 22 ♗xd4 ♘e6 23 ♕e3 ♕xc4 24 ♗b6 ♕xc2 25

0-0 ♕xe4 26 ♕xe4 ♗xe4 27 ♖xa5 ♖b8 28 ♗a7 ♖a8 29 ♗b6 ♖b8 'with a very unclear position' according to Beim. In our opinion it seems to be a just a draw by repetition of moves.

17 ...	♘c5
18 0-0	0-0
19 ♗d4?!	

White wastes two tempi to exchange his good bishop, but alternatives are difficult to see.

19 ...	♖fd8
20 ♗xc5	♕xc5
21 ♖fd1	g6

22 ♗e2	♘g7

Black is a pawn down but his position is overwhelming.

23 ♖xd8+	♖xd8
24 ♖d1	♖xd1+
25 ♕xd1	♘e6
26 h4?!	♔g7
27 h5	♗xe4
28 ♕d2	b3
	0-1

White resigned a little prematurely, but his position was lost in any case. In the next game White also stumbles over the Noteboom.

Game 23
Gallego – Bellon Lopez
Alicante 1989

(1 d4 d5 2 c4 e6 3 ♘c3 c6 4 ♘f3 dxc4 5 a4 ♗b4 6 e3 b5 7 ♗d2 a5 8 axb5 ♗xc3 9 ♗xc3 cxb5 10 b3 ♗b7 11 bxc4 b4 12 ♗b2 ♘f6 13 ♗d3 ♘bd7)

14 0-0	♕c7
15 ♖e1	0-0

16 e4

After 16 c5 Black can blockade the centre with 16...♗e4. In the game Malaniuk-Raičević, Kecskemet 1989, Raičević equalized after the somewhat strange move sequence 17 ♗b5 ♖fb8 18 ♗a4 ♖d8

19 ♘d2 ♗c6 20 ♕e2 ♗xa4 21 ♖xa4 e5.

16	...	e5
17	♘xe5	♘xe5
18	dxe5	♘d7

19 ♕h5

This position is favourable for Black. We give two examples of 19 f4 ♘c5 20 ♗c2 ♖fd8, White's major alternative to the text continuation:

- 21 ♕e2 a4 22 ♕e3 a3 23 ♗d4 ♖xd4 24 ♕xd4 b3 25 ♗d1 b2 26 ♖b1 a2 27 ♕xb2 ♘d3 0-1 (Van Bergen-Van der Werf, The Hague 1994).
- 21 ♕g4 a4 22 e6 fxe6 23 ♗e5 ♕f7 24 ♕e2 b3 25 ♗b1 a3 26 ♕e3 ♕e7 27 ♗d4 ♖xd4 28 ♕xd4 a2 0-1 (Ghijsen-Pliester, Amsterdam 1981).

19	...	♘c5
20	♖e3	♖fd8
21	♖h3	h6
22	♗c2	♖d2

Black is not afraid of ghosts and decides to take some material. Although his kingside will be ruined

his material advantage proves to be enough to win the game.

23	e6	♖xc2
24	♗e5	♕e7
25	♗xg7	♕xe6
26	♗xh6	♘xe4
27	♗g5	♕e5
28	♕h7+	♔f8
29	♗h6+	♔e7
30	♖d1	♖d8
31	♖e1	♖e2
32	♖f1	♘f6
33	♕g7	♖g8

0-1

Again White's play was far from perfect. In both of the previous games Black preferred 14...♕c7. We must stress that move order, Black's in particular, is important. The next few games show some serious attempts to put Black into trouble. The first attempt is 15 ♘d2 intending 15...0-0 16 f4 and White is in command. These games show that Black must immediately hit the centre with 15...e5, obtaining sufficient counterplay.

Game 24
Oei – Van der Werf
Wijk aan Zee 1994

(1 d4 d5 2 c4 c6 3 ♘c3 e6 4 ♘f3 dxc4 5 a4 ♗b4 6 e3 b5 7 ♗d2 a5 8 axb5 ♗xc3 9 ♗xc3 cxb5 10 b3 ♗b7 11 bxc4 b4 12 ♗b2 ♘f6 13 ♗d3 ♘bd7 14 0-0 ♕c7)

15 ♘d2   e5

Here 15...0-0 is a serious mistake on account of the reply 16 f4, when there is no way to prevent e4-e5. Vilela-Ruban, Santa Clara 1991, went 16...a4 17 ♖c1 ♖fd8 18 ♕e2 ♘f8 19 e4 b3 20 ♘b1 ♕b6 and now 21 e5 would have led to a clear advantage for White. Another example of the perils of this line (in which the move order was 14...0-0 15 ♘d2 ♕c7? 16 f4 a4) is the game Van der Werf-Cu. Hansen, Reykjavik 1996: 17 ♖b1 ♖fd8 18 ♕e2 ♖ab8 19 e4 ♘e8 20 ♖f3 ♗a8 21 ♖g3!? and Black found himself in big trouble.

16 ♖e1

16 f3 0-0 17 ♕c2 ♖e8 leads to the game Ionov-Volkov, Novgorod open 1995. After the continuation 18 c5 ♗c6 19 ♘c4 exd4 20 ♗xd4 a4 Black's queenside majority proved stronger than White's middlegame initiative.

16 ...   0-0
17 ♘f1   ♖fe8!

This is the natural square for the king's rook in the Noteboom variation. The naive trick 17...a4 fails to 18 dxe5 ♘xe5 19 ♗xe5 ♕xe5 20 ♖xa4.

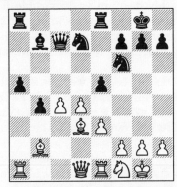

18 f3

Perhaps 18 ♘g3, first tried in the game Pia Cramling-Gdanski, Österskär 1995, is a better move. The position was unclear after 18...a4! 19 ♖b1 (not 19 ♖xa4?? ♕c6) 19...b3 20 ♗a3. Black's position would have been fine after 19...e4 20 ♗e2 ♕a5.

18	...	e4
19	♗e2	exf3
20	gxf3	♘h5!

This precise move prevents ♘g3 which would have given White a perfect position on account of his massive centre. Now his king position looks rather draughty and Black has a powerful initiative.

21 d5?!

White played the other pawn move, 21 c5, in Hoeksema-Van der Werf, Amsterdam 1994, but he resigned after 21...♖e6 22 ♗d3 ♕d8 23 ♕e2?? ♘f4 24 ♕d2 ♘xd3 25 ♕xd3 ♘e5! Black is also on the edge of victory after 23 ♘g3 ♘xg3 24 hxg3 ♕g5 25 ♔f2 ♕h6! The only move is 23 ♕c2, after which White can still fight.

21 ...   ♘c5?

Black must be very careful, as now he allows White to free himself. He could have maintained some advantage with 21...♖a6! 22 ♗d3 ♘e5 23 f4 ♘xd3 24 ♕xd3 ♖g6+ 25 ♔h1 ♕e7 intending 26 f5 ♖g4.

22 ♗d4?

White returns the favour. He could have seized the initiative with 22 f4! ♘f6 23 ♗f3 followed by ♘g3, ♗e5 and e3-e4.

22	...	♖a6
23	♗d3	♘xd3
24	♕xd3	♖g6+
25	♔h1	♕d8
26	♕d2	

26 ...   ♗a6?

That is not the place to be, because the pawn on c4 proves to be untouchable. Both 26...♗c8 27 ♕f2 and 26...♕h4 27 ♖xa5 are fine for White. The immediate 26...f5! is better for Black.

27 ♖ec1   f5

White wins after 27...♗xc4? 28 ♖xc4 ♕xd5 29 ♕e2 ♘f4? 30 exf4.

28	♕f2	f4
29	e4	♖h6
30	e5	♕g5

Threatening ...♘g3+!

31 ♕d2   ♗c8!

Black spends several moves forcing the e-pawn to e6. White's centre is impressive, but vulnerable.

32	e6	♗b7

33 ♕d3?

This passive move puts White into trouble. His e-pawn is lost in any case, so he should grab one himself. After 33 ♖xa5 ♖exe6 34 ♖a7 ♖e7 35 ♗c5! (35 ♖e1 ♘g3+ 36 ♘xg3 fxg3 37 ♕xg5 ♖xh2+ 38 ♔g1 ♖xe1 mate or 35 ♖b1 ♕f5 36 ♖xb4 ♘g3+ with a decisive attack) White is in command. So Black should play 33...♖hxe6 34 ♖a2 ♘f6! Now White has four possibilities: 35 ♕xb4 ♖e2 loses at once, 35 ♗xf6 ♖xf6 36 ♕xb4 ♖g6 37 ♕c5 ♖c8 followed by ...♗xd5 is awkward, 35 ♘g3 ♗xd5 36 cxd5 ♕xd5 is also problematic, and finally 35 ♖b2 ♘xd5! 36 cxd5 ♗xd5 37 ♕d3 ♕g4 38 ♖f2 ♖e2 39 ♘d2 ♖xd2 40 ♕xd2 ♗xf3+ leads to an equal position in which Black can try for more.

33	...	♖exe6!
34	♖c2	

Black's attack is decisive after 34 dxe6 ♘g3+ 35 ♔g1 ♘xf1+ 36 ♔xf1 ♖xh2.

34	...	♖e8
35	♖g2	♕d8
36	♘d2	♗c8
37	♘e4	♗h3
38	♖g5	♖g6?!

Both players were in time-trouble here. Black should have played 38...♘g3+! 39 ♔g1 ♘f5 40 ♔h1 ♖xe4 41 ♕xe4 ♘xd4 42 ♖ag1 ♘f5 43 ♖xf5 ♗xf5 44 ♕xf5 ♖f6 45 ♕g5 ♕f8 in order to secure his advantage.

39 ♖xh5??

This blunder abruptly finishes the game. After 39 ♖xg6 hxg6 or 39 ♖ag1 ♘g3+ 40 hxg3 ♖xg5 41 ♘xg5 ♕xg5 42 gxf4 ♕xf4 43 ♗xg7 ♗f5 44 ♗e5+ ♔f8 45 ♗xf4 ♗xd3, Black has only a slight edge.

39	...	♗g2+
40	♔g1	♗xf3+

0-1

Another try in this variation is to play 16 f4 anyway. In the following game Black easily seizes the initiative.

Game 25
Grooten – R.Kuijf
Rotterdam 1995

(1 d4 d5 2 c4 e6 3 ♘f3 c6 4 ♘c3 dxc4 5 a4 ♝b4 6 e3 b5 7 ♝d2 ♝b7 8 axb5 ♝xc3 9 ♝xc3 cxb5 10 b3 a5 11 bxc4 b4 12 ♝b2 ♘f6 13 ♝d3 ♘bd7 14 0-0 ♕c7 15 ♘d2 e5)

16 f4

Or 16 dxe5 ♘xe5 17 ♕a4+ ♘fd7 18 ♝e4 (18 ♝f5 0-0 19 f4 ♝c6 20 ♕c2 ♘g6) 18...0-0 19 c5 ♘xc5 20 ♕c2 ♘g4 21 g3 ♝xe4 22 ♘xe4 ♘e6 23 ♕e2 ♘h6 and White's compensation is insufficient.

16 ...	exd4
17 exd4	0-0
18 d5	♖fe8

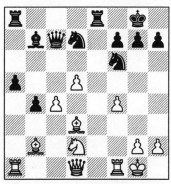

Black has a very pleasant position, since he controls the e-file and the important c5 square. Moreover, his queenside pawns are a valuable asset for the endgame. As usual in the Noteboom variation, White tries to avoid an endgame by attacking in the centre and on the kingside.

19 ♝d4	♘c5
20 ♝f5	♕d6
21 ♘f3	a4
22 ♘e5	♝c8!

White's pieces look impressive, but this cool retreat neutralizes any danger. White has to swap, because 23 ♝b1 is not what he intended when he played ♝f5.

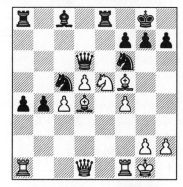

23 ♝xc8	♖exc8
24 ♘c6	♖xc6!

Of course, the knights dominate the rooks.

25 ♝e5	♕d7
26 dxc6	♕xc6 *(D)*
27 ♕d6?	

27 ♕c2 was absolutely essential. Now White faces a typical Noteboom endgame in which Black's queenside pawns are irresistible.

| 27 ... | ♕xd6 |

28	♗xd6	♘fe4
29	♗xc5	♘xc5
30	♖fb1	b3
31	♔f2	♔f8
32	♔e3	♖d8

33 ♖a3

White decides to stop the passed pawns, since after 33 ♖d1 ♖xd1 34 ♖xd1 a3, both 35 ♔d4 ♘a4 or 35 ♔d2 ♘e4+ lead to a new black queen. However, Black's advantage is decisive anyway.

33...♖d3+ 34 ♔e2 ♖c3 35 ♖d1 ♖xc4 36 g3 ♖c2+ 37 ♔e3 ♔e7 38 h4 ♖c4 39 g4 ♖e4+ 40 ♔f3 ♖c4 41 ♔e3 g6 42 ♖d2 ♖c3+ 43 ♔e2 ♖h3 44 ♖d5 ♖h2+ 45 ♔e3 b2 0-1

The best move after 14 0-0 ♕c7, however, is 15 d5!, after which Black cannot equalize, as we see in the next game.

Game 26
Novik – Karasev
St Petersburg 1994

(1 d4 d5 2 c4 e6 3 ♘c3 c6 4 ♘f3 dxc4 5 e3 b5 6 a4 ♗b4 7 ♗d2 a5 8 axb5 ♗xc3 9 ♗xc3 cxb5 10 b3 ♗b7 11 bxc4 b4 12 ♗b2 ♘f6 13 ♗d3 ♘bd7 14 0-0 ♕c7)

15 d5! *(D)*

Perfectly logical! Black delays castling and White takes advantage of the omission. His main idea is 15...exd5 16 cxd5 ♗xd5 (16...♘xd5 17 ♗xg7 ♖g8 18 ♖c1 ♕d6 19 ♗d4 and Black is suffering) 17 e4 ♗c6 18 ♖c1 ♕b7 19 ♘g5 and White's initiative outweighs the sacrificed pawn.

15	...	e5
16	e4	0-0
17	c5?!	

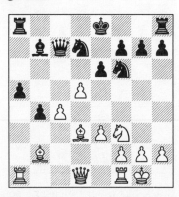

Much better is 17 ♖c1! with a substantial advantage, since Black cannot prevent c4-c5. In the game Black is able to equalize.

| 17 | ... | ♕xc5 |
| 18 | ♘xe5 | ♘xe5 |

19	♗xe5	♗a6
20	♗xf6	

White must act quickly, otherwise Black seizes the advantage, e.g. 20 ♖e1 ♗xd3 21 ♕xd3 a4.

20	...	gxf6
21	♕g4+	♔h8
22	♕h4	♗xd3

Black cannot avoid draw because both 22...♕d4 23 ♖ad1 ♕e5

24 f4 and 22...♕e7 23 ♖ad1 ♗xd3 24 ♖xd3 ♖g8 25 ♖fd1 a4 26 e5 are risky.

23	♕xf6+	½-½

We have now seen that 14...♕c7 allows White to take the initiative. The next game shows that it is not necessary to move the queen to prepare ...e6-e5.

Game 27
Forgo – Scholten
Correspondence game 1986-87

(1 d4 d5 2 c4 c6 3 ♘c3 e6 4 ♘f3 dxc4 5 a4 ♗b4 6 e3 b5 7 ♗d2 ♗b7 8 axb5 ♗xc3 9 ♗xc3 cxb5 10 b3 a5 11 bxc4 b4 12 ♗b2 ♘f6 13 ♗d3 ♘bd7 14 0-0)

14	...	0-0
15	♘d2	e5!

A strong pawn sacrifice that prevents f2-f4.

16	dxe5

16 d5, as played in the game Rossiter-Muir, British championship,

Dundee 1993, does not look good. After 16...♘c5 17 ♗f5 ♕d6 followed by ...a5-a4 Black has a dream position.

16	...	♘xe5
17	♗xh7+	

Black has good prospects after 17 ♗xe5 ♕xd3 18 ♗xf6 ♕g6.

17	...	♘xh7
18	♗xe5	♕g5
19	♗g3	♖fd8
20	♕c2	

Or 20 ♕e2 a4 21 ♘f3 ♕g4!

20	...	a4
21	♖fb1	♕c5 (D)

The outcome of the pawn sacrifice is tremendous for Black, because his passed pawns are getting serious, his bishop and queen are active and his knight will soon return to the battlefield to attack the king.

22	♕b2	b3
23	♖d1	♗c6
24	♕c3	♕f5

25 ♘f1   ♖xd1
26 ♖xd1   ♘g5

Watch out for 27...♘h3+ 28 ♔h1 ♕f3!

27 ♘d2   ♖d8
28 ♖c1   ♕d7
29 ♕d4

This loses at once, but 29 ♘f1 ♕b7 30 f3 a3 is also hopeless.

29 ...   ♕xd4
30 exd4   b2
31 ♖f1   a3

32 d5   f6!
The quickest way to victory.

33 dxc6   a2
0-1

Returning to the question of move-order, we conclude that Black does better to castle first to prevent White from getting aggressive ideas. His position is then solid enough to maintain the balance.

7 White does not play 16 e4 in the main line

The main line of the Noteboom occurs after White has played 0-0 and ♕d1-c2 on moves 14 and 15, and Black has copied these moves. In general White then plays 16 e4 to start his activities in the centre. In this chapter we look at positions in which White deviates by playing 16 c5 or 16 ♘e5. After 16 c5 Black is not forced to answer e3-e4 with ...e6-e5 because he has the excellent d5 square for his knight if White plays e4-e5. A good reply is 16...h6 anticipating the advance of the white e-pawn. On 16 ♘e5 Black is happily forced to play a strong pawn sacrifice. Neither system gives White much chance of gaining an opening advantage.

Game 28
Van Wely – Serper
Helsinki open 1992

(1 d4 d5 2 c4 e6 3 ♘c3 ♗b4 4 ♘f3 dxc4 5 e3 b5 6 a4 c6 7 ♗d2 a5 8 axb5 ♗xc3 9 ♗xc3 cxb5 10 b3 ♗b7 11 bxc4 b4 12 ♗b2 ♘f6 13 ♗d3 ♘bd7 14 ♕c2 0-0 15 0-0 ♕c7)

    16 c5!? *(D)*
    16 ...   h6

Anticipating e3-e4-e5. 16...♗a6!? to swap the light-squared bishops is a solid alternative here. For example, after 17 ♗xa6 ♖xa6 18 e4 ♖fa8 19 e5 ♘d5 20 ♘g5 ♘f8 21 ♕a4 ♘g6 22 g3 h6 23 ♘e4 ♘ge7 24 ♖a2 ♕c6 25 ♖fa1 ♕xa4 26 ♖xa4 ♘c6 both White's centre pawns and the black queenside pawns are permanently blocked, so there is no way to make progress for

either side. The game Kalantarian-Baburin, Kstovo open 1994, ended in a draw after a few more moves.

    17 e4   ♗c6!

If the white pawn advances to e5, the black knight can go to d5, so Black does not need to answer e3-e4 with ...e6-e5. Therefore he immediately prepares the advance of his queenside pawns. If Black plays 17...e5 we transpose to game 32.

    18 ♖fb1   **a4**
    19 ♗c1?

19 ♘d2 intending ♗c1, f2-f3, ♘c4, g2-g3, ♗f4 is the best set-up for White according to Serper.

    19 ...   **♖fb8?**

Black should have preferred 19...♕b7! intending to continue 20 ♘d2 b3! winning a pawn.

    20 ♘d2   **b3**
    21 ♕c3   **e5!**

The introduction to a powerful piece sacrifice.

    22 d5   **♗xd5!**
    23 exd5   **♘xd5**
    24 ♕c4   **♕xc5**

With three pawns and active pieces Black has very good compensation for the piece. The initial threat is 25...♘c3 26 ♖b2 ♘d1 27 ♖b1 b2 regaining the piece. White's next move is practically forced.

    25 ♗b2   **♘b4**
    26 ♗e4?!

White should have played 26 ♗f5, but after 26...♕xc4 27 ♘xc4 ♘c5 28 ♗xe5 ♖d8 Black has compensation for the sacrificed piece.

    26 ...   **♕xc4**
    27 ♘xc4   **♖a7?!**

Stronger was 27...♖a6 to meet 28 ♗f5 with 28...♘c5.

    28 ♗f5!   **♘c2!**

White can now meet 28...♘c5 by 29 ♗xe5 intending 30 ♗d6.

    29 ♗xc2   **bxc2**
    30 ♖c1   **♖c7**
    31 ♖xa4?   **♘b6?**

White's last move was a mistake, from which Black could have profited with 31...♘c5! with the threats 32...♘xa4, 32...♘d3, and 32...♘b3 followed by 33...♘d4. In a time scramble White proved to have the strongest nerves.

32	♘xb6	♖xb6
33	♖a2!	♖d7
34	♖f1	♖d2?!
35	♗c1	♖e2
36	♗e3	♖d6
37	♖aa1	f5
38	♖fc1	f4

39	♔f1	♖d1+
40	♖xd1	cxd1♕+
	1-0	

Black lost on time while making his last move.

Instead of 16 c5 white players have tried to put Black's position under pressure with 16 ♘e5 followed by f2-f4 and a kingside attack. Black's best reply is seen in the next game where he sacrifices a pawn for promising compensation.

Game 29
Khomiakov – Sorokin
Katowice open 1992

(1 d4 d5 2 c4 e6 3 ♘f3 c6 4 ♘c3 dxc4 5 e3 b5 6 a4 ♗b4 7 ♗d2 a5 8 axb5 ♗xc3 9 ♗xc3 cxb5 10 b3 ♗b7 11 bxc4 b4 12 ♗b2 ♘f6 13 ♗d3 ♘bd7 14 ♕c2 ♕c7 15 0-0 0-0)

16 ♘e5

This continuation is harmless for Black if he is willing to play a perfectly sound pawn sacrifice. The knight move is also possible after the preparatory 16 ♖fe1 ♖fe8. For example 17 ♘e5 ♘xe5! (the same pawn sacrifice as in the game) 18 dxe5 ♘d7 19 ♗xh7+ ♔h8 20 ♗d3 ♘c5 21 ♗d4 a4 (Black already has more than enough compensation for the pawn) 22 ♗xc5 ♕xc5 23 f4 ♖ed8 24 ♕e2 g6 25 ♗b1 b3 26 h4 ♕b4 27 ♖d1 ♖xd1+ 28 ♕xd1 ♕c3 29 ♖xa4 ♕xe3+ 30 ♔h2

♕xf4+ 31 ♔h3 ♖xa4 32 ♗xg6 ♗xg2+ 0-1 (Shutler-Hergott, British championship, Swansea 1987).

16 ... ♘xe5!

The pawn sacrifice implied by the text move is definitely the best way for Black to continue. Other moves allow 17 f4, after which

White takes control of the centre. For example, 16...h6 17 f4 ♘xe5 18 fxe5 ♘d7 19 ♖f4 ♗c6 20 ♖af1 a4 21 d5, when White has a significant space advantage and will start a kingside attack.

17 dxe5   ♘d7
18 ♗xh7+   ♔h8

19 ♗e4

White players have also tried the piece sacrifice 19 ♖fd1 g6 20 ♗xg6 fxg6 21 ♕xg6 ♘c5 22 ♗d4 but without success. Black's best move is 22...♘b3!, when in Saeed-Pliester, Amsterdam 1982, play continued 23 ♕xe6 ♖g8? (better was 23...♕g7 24 ♕h3+ ♕h7 25 e6+

♘xd4 26 ♕xh7+ ♔xh7 27 ♖xd4 ♖fb8 and Black has a decisive advantage) and now White should have played 24 ♕f6+ with sufficient counterplay.

19 ...   a4!
20 ♗xb7   ♕xb7
21 ♖ad1

21 ♖xa4 is a serious mistake because of 21...b3! and Black wins, a standard finesse in the Noteboom variation. Best seems 21 ♗d4, when after 21...♕c6 (21...♖fb8!?) 22 f4 ♔g8 a draw was agreed in Hraček-Matlak, Czechia 1993.

21 ...   a3
22 ♖d4   g6
23 ♗a1   b3
24 ♕d3   ♘c5
25 ♖h4+   ♔g7
26 ♕d4

Intending 27 ♕f4 followed by 28 ♕h6+ or 28 ♕f6+, but Black can easily prevent this.

26 ...   ♖h8
27 ♖xh8   ♔xh8
28 ♕xc5   b2
29 ♕b5   ♕xb5
30 cxb5   ♖c8

0-1

8 The ultimate Noteboom main line

The position after 16 e4 is regarded as a basic position in the Noteboom variation. Black's only sensible answer is 16...e5 to stop the advance of the e-pawn. White must try to force Black to exchange on d4, then advance with e4-e5 and follow up with a kingside attack. Black waits for the right moment to take on d4, giving White an isolated c-pawn and using the c6 square for his bishop and c5 for his knight to support the advance of his passed pawns. In general endgames are very pleasant for Black, due to his passed pawns on the a- and b-files (the Noteboom 'twins'). White's best move is 17 ℤfe1 (games 33, 34 and 35), but you will also probably encounter 17 ♘xe5 (game 30) and 17 c5 (games 31 and 32) and practice. Both White and Black have to cope with the tricky question: 'Where to place the rooks?'. White has the difficult choice of selecting two of the three squares a1, c1 and e1. The answer for Black is very simple: 'Put them opposite the white rooks.'

Game 30
Sanchez Guirado – Bellon Lopez
Barcelona 1989

(1 d4 d5 2 ♘f3 e6 3 c4 c6 4 ♘c3 dxc4 5 a4 ♗b4 6 e3 b5 7 ♗d2 a5 8 axb5 ♗xc3 9 ♗xc3 cxb5 10 b3 ♗b7 11 bxc4 b4 12 ♗b2 ♘f6 13 ♗d3 ♘bd7 14 0-0 0-0 15 ♕c2 ♕c7)

| 16 e4 | e5 |
| 17 ♘xe5 (D) | |

This continuation does not pose Black serious problems. The antipositional 17 d5? ℤfe8 followed by ...♘c5 and ...a5-a4 is just as bad for White as it looks. Also unimpressive is 17 h3?! exd4 (17...ℤfe8 is stronger, because 18 dxe5 is answered by 18...♘h5) 18 ♗xd4 ♘h5!? (Black can also play 18...h6) 19 c5 ♘f4 20 ℤfc1 ♗c6 21 ♗c4 ♕b7 22 ℤe1 a4 23 ♘h4 ♘e6 24 ♗xe6 fxe6 25 ♕c4 ℤfe8 26 ♘f5! ♗b5 27 ♘d6 ♗xc4 28 ♘xb7 with an unclear position in the game Arbakov-Stangl, Berlin open 1993. White's pieces are temporarily more active, but Black's pawn duo is an 'eternal' danger.

| 17 ... | ♘xe5 |
| 18 dxe5 | ♘g4 |

18...♘d7 is also possible. In Kujawski-Matlak, Miedzybrodzie Zyw. 1991 Black gained a strong initiative after 19 f4 ♘c5 20 ♖f3 ♖fd8 21 ♖e1 a4 22 e6 ♘xe6 23 ♖g3 ♕xf4 24 ♖f1 ♕c7 25 ♕f2 ♖xd3! 26 ♖xd3 ♗xe4.

19 ♗e2   ♘xe5
20 f4   ♘d7

The best square for the knight, from where it is on its way to c5.

21 e5   ♘c5
22 f5

White has built up an impressive centre, but is hard for him to get it to work.

22 ...   a4

Black continues as if nothing is happening on his kingside. 23 e6 is answered by 23...f6 and 23 f6 is met by 23...a3 24 fxg7 ♖d8 25 ♗c1 ♕xe5.

23 e6   f6
24 ♗h5   ♘xe6!?

Also good is 24...a3 25 ♗f7+ ♔h8.

25 fxe6   ♕c5+
26 ♖f2   ♕xh5
27 ♖xa4   ♗e4

28 ♕b3   ♖xa4
29 ♕xa4   ♖d8
30 h3   ♕c5

Black has a superior position.

31 ♕b5   ♖d1+
32 ♔h2   ♕d6+
33 ♗e5   ♕xe6

Of course not 33...♕xe5 34 ♕xe5 fxe5 35 e7 and White wins. After the move played Black remains a pawn up.

34 ♗g3   ♖b1
35 ♖e2   h6
36 c5   b3
37 ♕b4   f5
38 ♕d4   ♕a6
39 ♖f2   b2!

White has no defence to Black's many threats.

40 ♖xb2   ♕f1
41 ♗e5   ♖d1
42 ♕f2   ♕h1+
43 ♔g3   ♖g1
44 ♔h4   ♖xg2
45 ♕e3   ♖g4+
46 ♔h5   ♗f3
47 ♖b8+   ♔f7
48 ♕b3+   ♖c4+

0-1

Game 30 demonstrates that the continuation 17 ♘xe5 does not give Black any trouble if he aims for active piece play, and does not get nervous of White's pawn front on the kingside. The next game shows the implications of an early c4-c5 by White.

Game 31
Jasnikowski – Sherbakov
Katowice open 1992

(1 d4 d5 2 c4 e6 3 ♘c3 c6 4 ♘f3 dxc4 5 e3 b5 6 a4 ♗b4 7 ♗d2 a5 8 axb5 ♗xc3 9 ♗xc3 cxb5 10 b3 ♗b7 11 bxc4 b4 12 ♗b2 ♘f6 13 ♗d3 ♘bd7 14 0-0 0-0 15 ♕c2 ♕c7 16 e4 e5)

17 c5   exd4

Black voluntarily exchanges on d4 thereby creating the possibility of ...♗b7-c6. The advance e4-e5 is no longer dangerous as Black can play ...♘f6-d5.

17...♗a6 to exchange the light-squared bishops was given a hard blow in Van Wely-Engedal, Gausdal 1993: 18 ♗xa6 ♖xa6 19 ♖fc1 ♖c6 (19...♖c8 20 d5! ♘xc5 21 ♗xe5 ♕b6 22 ♗d4 ♘fd7 23 e5 with a huge advantage) 20 dxe5! ♘g4 21 h3 ♖xc5 (forced because 21...♘gxe5 22 ♗xe5 ♘xe5 23 ♘xe5 ♕xe5 24 ♖xa5 is not playable for Black) 22 ♕d2 ♘h6 (22...♘gxe5? 23 ♘xe5 ♘xe5 24 ♕d4! and White wins, a manoeuvre to remember!) 23 ♖xc5 ♘xc5 24 ♖c1 ♕e7 25 ♕d5 ♘e6 (25...♘b7 26 ♘d4 with the advantage) 26 ♕xa5 and White had a big advantage.

However, 17...♖fe8 is playable, for example:

* 18 ♖fe1 transposes to games 33-35.

* 18 ♖fc1 ♖ec8 19 ♕e2 exd4 20 c6 ♗xc6 21 ♘xd4 ♕b7 22 e5 ♘d5 23 ♘f5 ♘f8 24 ♕g4 ♘e6 and Black was better in Wegner-Sorokin, Belgorod 1991.

* 18 ♖ac1 ♖ac8 19 ♖fe1 exd4 20 ♗xd4 h6 21 h3 ♗c6 22 e5 ♘d5 23 e6 ♖xe6 24 ♖xe6 fxe6 25 ♗h7+ ♔h8 26 ♗xg7+ ♔xg7 27 ♕g6+ ♔h8 28 ♗g8 (28 ♕xh6 ♕f4 29 ♘g5!? ♕xc1+ and Black wins) 28...♘f8 and Black was able to defend in Marchand-Stangl, Verdun 1993.

We discuss the interesting move 17...h6!? in game 32.

18 ♗xd4   h6

18...♗a6 19 e5 ♗xd3 20 ♕xd3 ♘h5 21 e6 is good for White, but 18...♘g4!? is an interesting alternative. For example:

- 19 ♖fc1 ♗c6 20 e5?! ♗xf3! 21 gxf3 ♘dxe5 22 ♗xh7+ ♚h8 23 ♗e4? (23 ♕f5! ♘xf3+ 24 ♕xf3 ♕xh2+ 25 ♚f1 ♕h4 26 ♚g2 with an equal position) 23...♖ad8 and Black was better in Nesterov-Relange, Groningen open 1993.
- 19 ♗b5 ♘de5 20 ♘xe5 ♘xe5 21 ♕b2 f6 22 ♗xe5 fxe5 23 c6 ♗c8 and Black had no problems in Züger-Klinger, Bern open 1991.

19 ♖fc1

19 ♖fe1 ♖fe8 will transpose to games 33-35.

19 ...   ♗c6!

Both preventing c5-c6 and supporting the advance of the black a-pawn.

20 e5

More solid is 20 ♕b2 ♖fe8 21 h3 (21 e5 is answered by 21...♘h5 rather than 21...♘d5 22 e6 ♖xe6 23 ♗xg7 ♘f4 24 ♗f5 ♖e2 25 ♕d4)

21...♖e6 (21...♘xe4 22 ♗xg7 and 21...♗xe4 22 ♗xe4 ♘xe4 23 ♗xg7 only give troubles) 22 ♘h4!? ♘e5?! (22...♗e4! is favourable for Black, according to Sherbakov) 23 ♗b1 ♘xe4!? 24 f4 ♘g6 25 f5 ♘xh4 (Black is forced to sacrifice the exchange) 26 fxe6 ♕g3 27 exf7+ ♚xf7 28 ♖f1+ ♚g8 29 ♕e2 ♖e8 (stronger seems 29...♘eg5! threatening 30...♘xh3+ and 30...♘gf3+) 30 ♕g4 ♘xg2! 31 ♖xa5 ♕xg4 32 hxg4 ♘g3 33 ♗a2+ ♚h7 34 ♗b1+ ♚g8 (if 34...♚h8, then 35 ♗xg7+!) 35 ♗a2+ ♚h7 36 ♗b1+ ♚g8 ½-½ Ikonnikov-Sherbakov, Chelyabinsk 1992.

20 ...	♘d5
21 ♗c4	♖fe8
22 ♕e4	♕b7
23 ♕g4	♖e6
24 ♘h4	♘xe5
25 ♗xe5	♖xe5
26 ♘f5	

White's attack looks dangerous, and Black has to return his pawn in order to defend his kingside. However, as a result of the complications Black has exchanged some pieces and this is clearly favourable for him.

26 ...	g6
27 ♘xh6+	♚h7
28 ♕d4	♖ae8
29 ♘g4	♖e4
30 ♘f6+	♘xf6
31 ♕xf6	♕e7!

Forcing further piece exchanges.

32 ♕xc6	♖xc4
33 h3	♖c3
34 ♖xc3	bxc3

35	♕a4	♖c8
36	c6	♕e6
37	♕h4+?	

White chooses the wrong plan in time-trouble. Swapping queens results in an easily winning rook ending for Black. With 37 ♕xa5 ♕xc6 38 ♖c1 c2 39 ♕d2 White could have provided more resistance.

37	...	♔g7
38	♕d4+	♕f6
39	♕xf6+	♔xf6
40	♖xa5	♖xc6
41	♖a1	c2
42	♖c1	♔e5
	0-1	

The prophylactic ...h7-h6 is quite common in the Noteboom main line and the next game features an early example of this move, which has three ideas. First it is a useful waiting move that keeps the tension, second White cannot grab the pawn on h7 anymore, and third it allows the knight manoeuvre ...♘f6-h7-f8-e6.

Game 32
Itkis – Matlak
Miedzybrodzie Zyw. 1991

(1 d4 d5 2 c4 e6 3 ♘f3 c6 4 ♘c3 dxc4 5 e3 b5 6 a4 ♗b4 7 ♗d2 ♗b7 8 b3 a5 9 axb5 ♗xc3 10 ♗xc3 cxb5 11 bxc4 b4 12 ♗b2 ♘f6 13 ♗d3 ♘bd7 14 ♕c2 0-0 15 0-0 ♕c7 16 e4 e5 17 c5)

17	...	h6!?

17...h6!? is a beneficial waiting move. Black no longer has to worry about the protection of h7, back-rank mates are prevented, and if White takes on e5 the knight from f6 can go to h7 (and then on to f8 and e6).

| 18 | ♖fc1 | |

18 dxe5 may transpose to the game. Other moves have not yet been played in tournament practice.

18	...	♖fc8
19	dxe5	♘h5

Alternatives are:

- 19...♘g4? 20 c6! ♗xc6 (20...♕xc6 21 ♕xc6 ♗xc6 22 h3 wins) 21 ♗b5 ♘gxe5 22 ♘xe5 ♘xe5 23 ♗xe5 ♕xe5 24 ♗xc6 ♖a6 25 ♕a4 and White wins.

- 19...♘h7!? (on its way to e6) 20 ♗d4 ♘hf8 21 ♗c4 ♘e6 22 ♗xe6 fxe6 23 ♕b3 ♖a6 24 ♕c4 ♖c6 25 ♕b5 ♘xc5! 26 ♖xc5 ♖xc5 27 ♗xc5 ♕xc5 28 ♕xb7 ♕c1+ 29 ♘e1 ♕xa1! 30 ♕xc8+ ♔h7 31 ♔f1 b3 32 ♕xe6 ½-½ H.Klarenbeek-R.Kuijf, Dutch championship, Eindhoven 1992

| 20 | ♕d2 | |

Threatening 21 g4. In Krasenkov-Volzhin, Katowice open 1992, White allowed 20...♘f4. After 20 ♗d4 ♘f4 21 ♗c4 ♕c6 22 ♗e3 Black played the incorrect piece sacrifice 22...♘xg2 23 ♔xg2 ♕g6+ 24 ♔f1 ♗xe4 25 ♕d1 ♖d8 26 ♘h4 ♕h7 27 ♕h5 and wins. Better is 22...♘e6, transposing to the game Klarenbeek-Kuijf from the previous note.

20 ...   ♘xc5!?

Moving into this self-pin leads to unfathomable tactical complications that turn out in Black's favour.

21 ♗d4   ♕e7

22 ♖xc5

Or 22 ♗xc5 ♖xc5 and now:
- 23 ♖xc5 ♕xc5 24 g4 ♖d8 25 gxh5 ♗xe4 26 ♗xe4 (26 ♘e1 ♕xe5 27 ♖d1 ♕xh5 is good for Black) 26...♖xd2 27 ♘xd2 ♕xe5 28 ♖c1 f5 and Black wins.
- 23 g4 ♖d8 24 gxh5 ♗xe4 25 ♗xe4 ♖xd2 26 ♘xd2 ♕xe5! and wins.

22 ...   ♖xc5
23 g4   ♕d7!?

23...♖cc8 24 gxh5 a4 25 ♔h1 a3 26 ♖g1 is very unclear. White's attack looks more promising than Black's passed pawns.

24 h3

Of course not 24 gxh5 ♕g4+ 25 ♔f1 ♕xf3 26 ♗xc5 ♕h1+ or, alternatively, 24 ♗xc5 ♕xg4+ 25 ♔f1 ♕xf3 with the threats of 26...♕h1+ and 26...♘f4.

24 ...   ♖c3!?
25 gxh5

After 25 ♗xc3 bxc3 26 ♕xc3 ♘f4 Black stands better.

25 ...   ♕xh3
26 ♗xc3   ♕xf3
27 ♗d4   ♖d8

Black regains the piece by force.

28 ♕e3   ♕g4+
29 ♔f1   ♕d7
30 ♔e2   ♕xd4
31 ♕xd4   ♖xd4
32 ♔e3   ♖d8
33 ♖xa5   ♗c6
34 ♖a6??

A terrible blunder during time-trouble. After 34 ♗c4! Itkis should have been able to hold his own.

34 ...   ♖xd3+

0-1

Kramnik's way of playing the main variation of the Noteboom

(19...h6!) in his game with Neverov was the start of a Black revival after a number of White victories. White finds a dangerous idea to start an attack with the pawn sacrifice e4-e5-e6, but Black defends accurately and manages to take the upper hand.

Game 33
Neverov – Kramnik
Soviet championship, Moscow 1991

(1 d4 d5 2 c4 c6 3 ♘f3 e6 4 ♘c3 dxc4 5 a4 ♗b4 6 e3 b5 7 ♗d2 a5 8 axb5 ♗xc3 9 ♗xc3 cxb5 10 b3 ♗b7 11 bxc4 b4 12 ♗b2 ♘f6 13 ♗d3 ♘bd7 14 ♕c2 0-0 15 0-0 ♕c7 16 e4 e5)
17 ♖fe1   ♖fe8

18 c5
18 dxe5 was played in Madsen-Engedal, Oslo 1994. There followed 18...♘g4 19 e6 ♖xe6 20 h3 ♘ge5 21 ♘d4 ♘xd3 22 ♕xd3 ♖g6 23 ♘b5 ♕c6 24 ♖ad1 ♘f8 and Black had a good position. White now played 25 ♕d5? overlooking 25...♖xg2+! 26 ♔xg2 ♕g6+ 27 ♔h2 ♗xd5 28 exd5 ♕c2 and Black wins immediately.

18 ...   exd4
18...♗a6 is also possible, for example 19 ♗xa6 ♖xa6 20 dxe5 (this move might not be the best one) 20...♘g4 21 ♖ed1 ♘gxe5 22 ♘xe5 ♘xe5 23 ♖d5 h6 24 h3 ♖ae6 with equal chances in the game Bellon Lopez-Flear, Bern open 1992.

ECO suggests the immediate 18...h6, but there is no tournament experience with this. It does seem worth a try, as play might become similar to game 32.

19 ♗xd4   h6!
Before this move was introduced into tournament practice by Vladimir Kramnik, Black played 19...♘g4 or 19...♗a6. In both cases White maintained a slight advantage. For example 19...♗a6 20 ♗xa6 ♖xa6 21 ♕c4! ♘b8?! 22 e5 ♘fd7 23 ♘g5 ♘f8 24 e6 fxe6 25 ♗e5 ♕b7 26 ♗d6 with a white advantage in Magerramov-Mikenas, correspondence game 1989.

20 h3?!
Better is the immediate 20 e5 as can be seen from the following two games.

20 ...   ♗c6
21 e5

21 ♘h4!? was played in Zanetti-Boll, correspondence game 1993, resulting in very complicated play after 21...a4 22 ♘f5 b3 23 ♕c1 ♘e5 24 ♗b1 ♖ad8 25 f4 ♘ed7 26 ♘d6 ♖e7 27 e5 ♘d5 28 f5. White's position looks fine, but Black eventually won the game.

21 ...   ♘d5
22 e6!

White has to play aggressively. After the quiet 22 ♕b2? ♘f8 Black is better.

22 ...   ♖xe6
23 ♖xe6   fxe6
24 ♗h7+

24 ♖e1 ♘f4 25 ♗e4 ♖f8 is satisfactory for Black.

24 ...   ♔h8
25 ♗xg7+!

But not 25 ♕g6? e5 and 25 ♘h4 ♘f8.

25 ...   ♔xg7
26 ♕g6+   ♔h8
27 ♕xh6   ♘f8
28 ♗f5+   ♘h7
29 ♗xh7   ♕xh7
30 ♕xe6   ♘e7

Black has to defend carefully and 30...♘e7 is the only move. After the continuation 30...♕g7 31 ♕xc6! ♕xa1+ 32 ♔h2 White has a dangerous attack. For example, 32...♖d8? 33 ♕h6+ ♔g8 34 ♕g5+ and wins.

31 ♘e5   ♕g7
32 g4   ♗d5?!

More precise is 32...♗e8 33 ♖d1 a4 with advantage for Black.

33 ♕xe7   ♕xe7
34 ♘g6+   ♔h7
35 ♘xe7   ♗e4!
36 ♖e1?

White's best defence was 36 f3! ♗c2! 37 ♘d5 b3 38 ♘c3 b2 39 ♖a2 b1♕+ 40 ♘xb1 ♗xb1 which is only a little better for Black.

36 ...   a4!
37 c6

37 ♖xe4 a3 38 ♖e1 a2 39 ♖a1 b3 is hopeless as well.

37 ...   a3
38 c7   b3
39 c8♕   ♖xc8
40 ♘xc8   b2
          0-1

Shortly after his game against Neverov, Kramnik had the opportunity to play the Noteboom with White against Sorokin. He improved on Neverov's play with the immediate pawn sacrifice 21 e6!, which is undoubtedly better than preparing it with 21 h3. Sorokin is surprised, and is not able to find the best defence over the board. On move 25 he misses a good chance to reach at least equality.

Game 34
Kramnik – Sorokin
Rybinsk 1991

(1 d4 d5 2 c4 e6 3 ♘c3 c6 4 ♘f3 dxc4 5 a4 ♗b4 6 e3 b5 7 ♗d2 a5 8 axb5 ♗xc3 9 ♗xc3 cxb5 10 b3 ♗b7 11 bxc4 b4 12 ♗b2 ♘f6 13 ♗d3 ♘bd7 14 ♕c2 0-0 15 e4 e5 16 0-0 ♖e8 17 ♖fe1 ♕c7 18 c5 exd4 19 ♗xd4 h6 20 e5 ♘d5)

21 e6! *(D)*

An improvement over 21 ♗e4, which led to victory for Black in the correspondence game Adolph-Scholten, 1989: 21...♘f8 22 ♘d2 ♘e6 23 ♘f3 (not a particularly impressive manoeuvre) 23...♖ed8 24 ♖ed1 a4! 25 h3 (25 ♖xa4? ♖xa4 26 ♕xa4 ♘xd4 27 ♘xd4 ♘c3 and Black wins) 25...♗c6 (Black is already much better) 26 ♕c4 ♘e7 27 ♗e3 ♖d1+ 28 ♖xd1 ♕b7 29 ♗xc6 ♘xc6 30 ♕a2 b3 31 ♕a3 ♕b4 32 ♗c1 ♕xa3 0-1.

21 ...	♖xe6
22 ♖xe6	fxe6
23 ♖e1	♘f4
24 ♗e4	♖c8
25 ♘e5!?	

Nowadays 25 g3 is considered more accurate. Game 35 deals with this continuation.

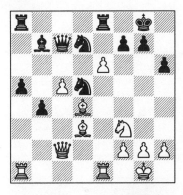

| 25 ... | ♗d5? |

A serious mistake. After the much better 25...♗xe4! 26 ♕xe4 ♘d5 27 ♘c4 (27 ♕g6 ♘7f6 or 27 ♘xd7 ♕xd7 28 ♕xe6+ ♕xe6 29 ♖xe6 b3 gives Black a slight plus) 27...♘xc5! 28 ♗xc5 ♕xc5 29 ♕xe6+ ♔h8 30 ♘d6? (30 ♘e5 was necessary) 30...♖f8 31 ♘f7 ♔h7 32 ♕f5 g6! 33 ♕d7 ♘f6! Black won in Obukhov-Sherbakov, Belorecheck 1992.

| 26 ♗h7+ | ♔f8 |
| 27 c6! | ♘xe5 |

27...♘f6 28 ♗c5+ ♔e8 29 ♗g6+ ♔d8 (29...♘xg6 30 ♕xg6+ ♔d8 is no better) 30 ♘f7+ and White wins.

28	♗xe5	♛xc6
29	♛xc6	♖xc6
30	♗xf4	

With a piece for two pawns, White has a winning position. In the rest of the game it is very instructive to see how White combines stopping Black's pawns with a mating attack.

30	...	a4
31	♖c1	♖b6
32	♖c7	a3
33	♗e3	♖b5

33...a2 34 ♗c5+ ♔e8 35 ♗g6+ ♔d8 36 ♗xb6 a1♛ 37 ♖c1+ and wins.

34	♗d3	♖a5
35	♗d4	b3

After 35...a3 36 ♗xg7+ ♔e8 37 ♗a1 Black's queenside pawns are blocked.

36	♗xg7+	♔g8
37	♗f6	b2
38	♗g6	♖a8
39	♖h7	

Black has to give up his queenside pawns to avoid mate. In return he regains his piece, but White's extra pawn and the weak black h-pawn secure the win.

39	...	b1♛+
40	♗xb1	a2
41	♖g7+	♔f8
42	♗xa2	♖xa2
43	h3	♗e4
44	♖e7	♖a6
45	♔h2	♗f5
46	g4	♗g6
47	♖g7	♗e4
48	♖c7	♔g8
49	♗d4	♗f3
50	♖g7+	♔f8
51	♖g6	♔e7
52	♖xh6	

The rest of the game is a matter of technique. We give the remaining moves without comment.

52...♗e4 53 ♔g3 ♖a4 54 ♗e3 ♗d3 55 ♗g5+ ♔d6 56 ♖h8 ♗e2 57 ♖d8+ ♔e5 58 ♗e7 ♖c4 59 ♔h4 ♖c3 60 ♖f8 ♔d5 61 ♗g5 ♖b3 62 ♗e3 ♖b1 63 ♔g5 e5 64 ♔f5 ♗d3+ 65 ♔f6 ♖h1 66 ♖h8 ♖a1 67 ♖d8+ ♔e4 68 h4 ♗e2 69 ♖g8 ♖a6+ 70 ♔g5 ♖a1 71 ♖b8 ♖a4 72 h5 ♔f3 73 ♖f8+ ♔g2 74

f4 ♔g3 75 h6 ♗d3 76 fxe5
♖xg4+ 77 ♔f6 ♔f3 78 e6 ♖g6+
79 ♔f7 1-0

In the following game Magerra-
mov improves upon Kramnik's
play with 25 g3 instead of 25 ♘e5,
which results in a balanced position with chances for both sides,

although in the game itself Sherbakov, one of the world's leading
Noteboom experts, seizes the initiative with a dynamic exchange
sacrifice. Current opening theory
considers that the position after
25...♘h3+ is the best both players
can achieve from the main line of
the Noteboom.

Game 35
Magerramov – Sherbakov
Moscow 1992

(1 d4 d5 2 c4 e6 3 ♘f3 c6 4 ♘c3
dxc4 5 a4 ♗b4 6 e3 b5 7 ♗d2 a5
8 axb5 ♗xc3 9 ♗xc3 cxb5 10 b3
♗b7 11 bxc4 b4 12 ♗b2 ♘f6 13
♗d3 ♘bd7 14 ♕c2 0-0 15 e4 e5
16 0-0 ♕c7 17 ♖fe1 ♖fe8 18 c5
exd4 19 ♗xd4 h6 20 e5 ♘d5 21
e6! ♖xe6 22 ♖xe6 fxe6 23 ♖e1
♘f4 24 ♗e4 ♖c8)
    25 g3!   **♘h3+** *(D)*
The only move since White wins
after both 25...♘d5? 26 ♗h7+ ♔h8
27 ♖xe6 (threatening 28 ♖h6+)
27...♘5f6 28 ♘h4! and 25...♘h5
26 c6!
    26 ♔f1
The game Van Wely-Dorfman,
Brussels zonal 1993, went 26 ♔g2
♘g5 27 ♘xg5 hxg5 28 ♔g1 ♗xe4
29 ♕xe4 ♕c6 30 ♕g6 e5 ½-½.
Black has no problems whatso-
ever.
    26 ...   **e5!?**
    27 ♘xe5   **♘xe5**
This continuation is more ambitious than 27...♗xe4 28 ♕xe4

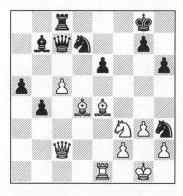

♘xe5 29 ♕xe5 ♘g5 30 ♕xc7 ♖xc7
31 ♖e8+ ♔f7 32 ♖a8, when the
game is drawish.
    28 ♗h7+
After 28 ♗xe5? ♗xe4! 29 ♖xe4
♕xc5 30 ♕xc5 ♖xc5 31 f4 g5! 32 f5
h5 Black has good winning chances.
    28 ...   **♔h8**
    29 ♗xe5   **♕f7**
Black is practically forced to
sacrifice the exchange, because after 29...♕xc5 30 ♗xg7+ ♔xg7 31
♕g6+ ♔h8 32 ♕f6+ ♔xh7 33
♖e7+ White wins.

30 &f5   ©g5

Not good is 30...b3 31 ♕d3 ♖f8 due to 32 g4! ©g5 33 ♖e3! threatening ♕b3 and f2-f4.

31 &xc8   &xc8

Black has sufficient compensation for the exchange. The light squares on White's kingside are terribly weak. The first threat is 32...&h3+ and wins.

32 ♖e3   ♕d5!
33 f3?

After 33 ♕d3! White holds the balance. For example 33...♕h1+ 34 ♔e2 &g4+ 35 f3 ♕h2+ 36 ♔e1 ♕g1+ 37 ♔e2 and Black has no more than perpetual check.

33 ...   ©xf3
34 &b2   &f5
35 ♕e2   ©d2+
36 ♔g1

On 36 ♔e1 Black also plays 36...©c4.

36 ...   ©c4
37 ♖e8+   ♔h7
38 &a1   b3
39 ♕f2   a4
40 &d4

40 ♖e7 is met by 40...b2, but now Black has to prevent this move.

40 ...   ♕d7
41 ♖b8   &e4
42 ♖b4   ©a5?

In time-trouble Black throws away the victory, which could be achieved with 42...♕d5! White has no defence against 43...©e5! forcing the exchange of the bishop, after which White cannot resist the advance of the black pawns.

43 ♕f4

White misses the chance to obtain a draw by 43 &b2!, threatening ♖xe4 and ♕d4. After 43...♕d1+ 44 ♕f1 ♕c2 45 ♕f2! ♕b1+ 46 ♕f1 the game should end in draw by repetition of moves.

43 ...   ♕b7

The game concluded 44 ♖b6 ♕d5 45 ♖xh6+ (a desperate and hopeless sacrifice, but White has no defence against Sherbakov's numerous threats) 45...gxh6 46 ♕c7+ ♔g6 47 ♕g7+ ♔f5 48 ♕h7+ ♔e6 49 ♕xh6+ ♔d7 50 c6+ &xc6 0-1

9 Anti-Noteboom systems: Marshall Gambit

The Marshall Gambit, 1 d4 d5 2 c4 e6 3 ♘c3 c6 4 e4, is one of the most popular methods of avoiding the Noteboom. This gambit usually leads to very dynamic games, in which Black is a pawn up but has to cope with an unsafe king position. White's results used to be very impressive, but recently Black has found ways to achieve a satisfactory position. The following game is a perfect example of White's possibilities in this gambit.

Game 36
Lautier – M.Gurevich
Biel interzonal 1993

1	c4	e6
2	♘c3	d5
3	d4	c6
4	e4	dxe4
5	♘xe4	♗b4+
6	♗d2	

If White does not wish to sacrifice a pawn he should play 6 ♘c3. In that case Black has the chance to invest a pawn with 6...e5. Although this gave Black sufficient compensation in Brkljaca-Todorović, Yugoslavia 1993, after 7 dxe5 ♕xd1+ 8 ♔xd1 ♗f5 9 ♘ge2 ♘d7 10 ♘g3 ♗g6 11 f4 ♘h6!, White should play 7 a3 ♗a5 8 dxe5 with a small plus. In fact, the best continuation for Black is 6...c5! 7 a3 ♗a5!? 8 ♗e3 ♘f6 with equal chances, as in Lerner-Lukacs, Polanica Zdroj 1986, after 9 ♘f3 ♘c6 10 dxc5 ♕xd1+ 11 ♖xd1 ♘e4 12 ♖c1 ♘xc3

13 bxc3 e5 14 ♘d2 ♗f5, or Groszpeter-Lukacs, Hungary 1991, after 9 ♖c1 cxd4 10 ♕xd4 ♕xd4 11 ♗xd4 ♘c6 12 ♗xf6 gxf6 13 b4 ♗c7.

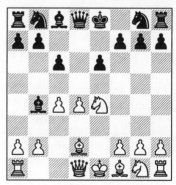

6	...	♕xd4
7	♗xb4	♕xe4+
8	♗e2	

The only reasonable alternative, 8 ♘e2, is the subject of game 39.

8 ...   ♘a6

Apart from 8...c5, which we will discuss in the next two games, Black has two other alternatives:

- 8...♘d7 9 ♘f3 c5 10 ♗c3 ♘gf6 11 ♕d6!? ♕g6 12 ♘d2! a5 13 0-0 ♖a6 14 ♕c7 0-0 15 ♗f3 was better for White in Stohl-Seitaj, Moscow 1994. Black cannot improve this variation as 10...f6 11 ♘d2! ♕f4 12 ♗h5+ g6 13 ♗f3 ♘e5 14 ♗e4 ♘f7 15 0-0 gave White the initiative in the game Dorfman-Ružele, Lyon 1994, and in this same line 11...♕c6 12 ♕xc6 bxc6 13 ♘d2 also gave Black a hard time in Zsu.Polgar-Kir.Georgiev, Pardubice 1994.

- 8...♘e7 is the first part of a knight manoeuvre that should lead to the f4 square. Grandmaster Khalifman showed an effective way to prevent this in his game against Filippov during the 1995 Russian championship: 9 ♕d2 (9 ♘f3 ♘d5!? 10 ♗a3 ♘f4 11 0-0! ♘xe2+ 12 ♔h1 ♘d7 13 ♖e1 ♕xc4 14 ♖xe2 c5 and White's compensation looks insufficient, Borisenko-Kalikstein, Uzhbekistan 1992) 9...♘g6 10 ♘h3! f6 11 0-0-0 ♔f7 12 f3 ♕h4 13 ♗c5 e5 14 ♘f2 f5 15 g3 ♕f6 16 ♖hf1!! and a few moves later ♘e4 was decisive.

9 ♗c3

White has also tried three other moves:

- 9 ♗f8?! looks spectacular but the cool 9...♕xg2 gives Black the better game. This reply is not possible after 8 ♘e2 ♘a6 9 ♗f8. Indeed, the notes to game 39 show that 9 ♗f8 is White's best move after 8 ♘e2 ♘a6.

- 9 ♗a5 looks odd. Black should avoid 9...b6? 10 ♗c3 ♘f6 11 ♕d6, but 9...♗d7 is a solid continuation. I.Sokolov-Sherbakov, Leeuwarden 1994, is worth examining: 10 ♘f3 ♘f6 11 ♕d6 ♕f5 12 ♘e5 ♕xf2+! 13 ♔xf2 ♘e4+ 14 ♔f3 ♘xd6 15 ♖hd1 ♔e7 16 ♖xd6!? ♔xd6. In this position White decided to play for mate with 17 ♖hd1+? ♔e5 18 ♗c3+ ♔f5 19 ♖d7 ♔g6 20 ♗d3 but after 20...♔g5! there was no mate and Black went on to win. Instead White should have regained the exchange with 17 ♘xf7+, leading to an approximately equal position.

- 9 ♗d6!? is unclear after 9...f6 10 ♘f3 e5 11 0-0 ♗e6.

9 ...   ♘e7

If Black wants to avoid the ensuing complications, he has an interesting alternative in 9...f6.

10 ♗xg7

This is better than the gambit style 10 ♘f3 0-0 11 0-0 f6 12 ♖e1. After 12...♘g6 13 b4 e5 Black had excellent chances in Lalić-Sherbakov, Hastings 1994.

10 ...   ♖g8

11 ♗f6

A useful stop on the journey to c3 as the immediate 11 ♗c3 gives Black the opportunity to grab the initiative with 11...♘d5. After 12 cxd5 ♕xg2 13 dxe6 ♗xe6 14 ♗f6

Black can sacrifice his queen with 14...♖g6!? 15 ♗h4 ♕xh1 16 ♕d6 ♕xg1+ 17 ♔d2 ♕g5+ 18 ♗xg5 ♖xg5 according to Romanovski. We agree that Black has abundant compensation.

11 ...   ♕f4

11...♖g6 is a logical and viable alternative. If White takes on e7, Black has no problems, for example 12 ♗xe7 ♔xe7 13 ♕d2 e5 14 ♖d1 ♗e6, Vaiser-Savchenko, Moscow 1992. Better is 12 ♗c3, as in the game Berg-Sherbakov, Cappelle la Grande 1995, which continued 12...♕xg2 13 ♕d2 (13 ♕d4? e5 14 ♕d2 ♕xh1 15 0-0-0 ♗f5 is an unfortunate idea of Glek's, from his game against Neverov, Tallinn 1986) 13...♕xh1 14 0-0-0 ♘d5 15 ♘f3 ♕g2 16 cxd5 cxd5 17 ♘e5 ♗d7 18 ♕f4 and White's attack was irresistible. Black played more solidly in the game Williams-Bryson, Hastings 1995: 12...e5 13 ♘f3 ♖xg2 14 ♕d2 f6 and had no problems after the opening.

12 ♗c3!

This pawn sacrifice is the best way to play for a win. The alternative 12 ♗xe7 ♔xe7 usually leads to an equal position, as in Sherbakov-Novikov, St Petersburg 1995: 13 g3 ♕e5 14 ♕b1 b6 15 ♘f3 ♕f6 16 0-0 ♗b7 17 ♕e4 ♘c5 18 ♕e3 ♘d7 19 ♗d3 c5.

12 ...   ♖xg2
13 ♘f3   f6

Lautier's analysis of this game shows that Black cannot achieve equality with any of the following four alternatives. White's advantage varies from large to decisive after either:

- 13...♘c5 14 ♗e5 ♕h6 15 ♕d4 b6 16 ♖d1 ♗b7 17 ♗f6! followed by 18 b4.
- 13...♘f5 14 ♗e5 ♕h6 15 ♕d2! ♖g8 (or 15...♕xd2+ 16 ♘xd2 ♖g6 17 ♘e4) 16 ♗f4 ♕f8 17 0-0-0 ♕e7 18 ♖hg1.
- 13...♗d7 14 ♗e5 ♕h6 15 ♗g3 ♘f5 16 ♕d2! or
- 13...♘g6 14 ♔f1 e5?! 15 ♔xg2 ♗h3+ 16 ♔xh3 ♕f5+ 17 ♔g2 ♘f4+ 18 ♔f1 ♕h3+ 19 ♔e1 ♘g2+ 20 ♔d2 ♖d8+ 21 ♔c2 ♖xd1 22 ♖axd1 ♘f4 23 ♖he1 ♘xe2 24 ♖xe2 ♕xf3 25 ♖xe5+ ♔f8 26 ♖d8+.

14 ♕d2!
White is not afraid to exchange queens, because his attack gains strength after the removal of the strongest defender. 14 ♕d3 would have allowed Black to equalize with 14...e5 15 ♕xh7 ♗g4! 16 ♗d2 ♕f5 17 ♕xf5 ♘xf5 18 h3 ♗xf3 19 ♗xf3 ♖g7.

14 ...   ♕xd2+

Other methods of exchanging queens do not improve Black's situation, because both 14...♘g6 15 ♕xf4! ♘xf4 16 ♗xf6 ♘xe2 17 ♔xe2 and 14...e5 15 ♕xf4 exf4 16 ♘h4! ♖g8 17 ♗h5+ ♘g6 18 0-0-0 ♔f7 19 ♖d6 ♗e6 20 ♖e1 followed by 21 ♘f5 are unpleasant.

15 ♘xd2   e5

And not 15...f5 16 ♗h5+ ♘g6 17 ♘f3 ♔e7 18 ♔f1 ♘f4 19 ♗e5, when White has a decisive advantage.

16 ♘e4   ♔f7
17 ♖d1!   ♖g8?!

Black's best defence was to play 17...♘c7, although he still has problems after 18 ♗h5+ ♘g6 19 ♗f3 ♘h4 20 ♗xg2 ♘xg2+ 21 ♔e2 ♘f4+ 22 ♔f3 ♗h3 23 ♖hg1 h5 24 ♔e3.

18 f4   ♘g6

Both 18...exf4 19 ♗h5+ ♘g6 20 ♘xf6 and 18...♗f5 19 ♘d6+ ♔e6 20 ♘xb7 ♖ab8 21 ♖d6+ ♔f7 22 ♘a5 are impossible.

19 ♖d6!

Look how easily White's attack progresses. Black loses the pawn on f6 because 19...♗e6 fails to 20 f5.

19 ...   ♔e7
20 ♖xf6   ♘xf4

Or 20...exf4 21 h4.

21 ♗xe5   ♘xe2
22 ♗d6+!   ♔e8
23 ♔xe2   ♗h3

On 23...♗g4+ White has 24 ♔e3, ♖d8 25 ♖g1!

24 ♖h6!   ♗g4+
25 ♔e3   ♗f5

25...♔f7 fails to 26 ♖f6+! ♔e8 27 ♖g1, so White wins the exchange on g8. The technical phase poses no problems for the Frenchman.

26 ♘f6+   ♔f7
27 ♘xg8   ♖xg8
28 ♔f4!   ♗g6
29 ♖e1   ♖d8
30 ♖e7+   ♔f6
31 c5   ♘b4
32 ♖exh7   ♘d5+
33 ♔f3   ♖e8
34 h4   ♖e3+
35 ♔f2   ♔f5
36 ♖g7   ♖e6

Or 36...♗e8 37 ♖g5+ ♔e4 38 ♖e6+ ♔d4 39 ♖xd5+.

37 h5

And, in view of 37...♗e8 38 ♖xe6 ♔xe6 39 h6, Black resigned.

1-0

The next two games feature 8...c5 instead of 8...♘a6. Although Black only scores one draw in these two games, the positions after the opening are fine for him.

Game 37
Hjartarson – Van der Werf
Reykjavik open 1996

1	c4	e6
2	♘c3	d5
3	d4	c6
4	e4	dxe4
5	♘xe4	♗b4+
6	♗d2	♕xd4
7	♗xb4	♕xe4+
8	♗e2	c5
9	♗xc5	♕xg2

10 ♗f3

This is probably White's best choice. Other moves allow Black to equalize at least:

- 10 ♕d6 ♘d7 11 ♗f3 (11 0-0-0 ♕c6! 12 ♗a3 ♕xd6 13 ♖xd6 ♘gf6 leads to a balanced position, Gulko-Weldon, New York 1987) 11...♕g5 12 ♗e3 ♕a5+ 13 ♔f1?! (better is the continuation 13 b4 ♕e5 14 ♕d4 ♘e7 15 ♗e4 ♘c6 with equal chances) 13...♘e7 14 ♗d2 ♕c5 15 ♕xc5 ♘xc5 and Black is better, as the

game Dybala-Maliutin, Wizla 1992, showed.
- 10 ♕d4 ♘d7! (not 10...♕xh1? 11 ♕xg7 with advantage to White) 11 0-0-0 ♕g5+ 12 f4 ♕f6! 13 ♘f3 ♘xc5 14 ♕xc5 ♕xf4+ 15 ♘d2 ♘f6!? 16 ♖hg1 ♗d7 17 ♖xg7 ♗c6 18 b4 ♖d8 19 b5 is Shishkin-Moroz, Dniepropetrovsk 1994. Instead of 14...♕xf4+ Black could have secured a substantial advantage with 14...♘e7! followed by ...0-0 or later with 18...♘e4! 19 ♕d4 ♖d8.
- 10 ♕d2?! ♕xh1! 11 0-0-0 ♘d7 12 ♘f3 ♕g2! (this looks natural but 12...♕xd1 has often been played) 13 ♗a3 (13 ♘e5 ♘gf6 14 ♕d6 ♕g5 15 f4 ♕xf4+ 16 ♔b1 ♘g8! is winning for Black. Also good is 15...♘e4!) and now Black's most convincing move is 13...♕xf2!, for instance 14 ♘e5 ♕xh2 15 ♘xd7 ♕h6 16 ♗f8 ♗xd7!

10	...	♕g5
11	♗d6	

An interesting alternative to this usual move is 11 ♗e3. In the game Gokhale-Imocha, Calcutta 1996, White had a pleasant initiative after 11...♕a5+ 12 ♗d2 ♕c7 13 ♗c3 ♘f6 14 ♘e2 ♘bd7 15 ♖g1 ♖g8 16 ♕a4 ♔f8 17 0-0-0 a5 18 ♖g5 e5 19 ♕a3+. An improvement for Black is 15...0-0 although White has some compensation for the pawn. A second alternative is 11 ♕d4 which was played in the game Vaiser-S.Ivanov, Uzhgorod 1988. That game went 11...♘d7 12 ♗b4 ♕e5+ 13 ♘e2 ♕xd4 14 ♘xd4 ♘e5 15 ♗e2 ♗d7 and now 16 ♗d6 instead of 16 ♖g1?! ♘e7! would have given White sufficient compensation.

11 ...   ♘e7

The commonly played 11...♘c6 unnecessarily gives White the extra option of 12 ♗xc6+. In Vaiser-Ermenkov, Odessa 1977, White had a slight edge after 12...bxc6 13 ♘f3 ♕a5+ 14 b4 ♕f5 15 ♕e2 ♘f6 16 ♖g1 ♗a6 17 ♖xg7 ♗xc4 18 ♕xc4 ♕xf3 19 ♗e5 ♘d7 20 ♗b2.

12 ♘e2

In his game against Monin in the Soviet Union 1980, Vladimirov tried 12 ♘h3 and obtained some compensation after 12...♕f6 13 ♖g1 ♘f5 14 ♗a3 ♕e5+ 15 ♔f1 ♘c6 16 ♕d3 ♕d4 17 ♗xc6 bxc6 18 ♕e2, but this plan looks suspicious. It is better to have the knight in the centre rather than the king.

12 ...   ♘bc6

White can launch an attack after 12...0-0 13 ♖g1 ♕f6 14 ♘g3.

13 ♖g1   ♕a5+

The usual move here is 13...♕f6, when 14 ♘c3 leaves Black with a difficult choice. After 14...♘f5?! 15 ♗xc6+ bxc6 16 ♘e4 ♕d8 17 ♕d2 ♗a6 18 b3 White has a clear edge, as the game Spraggett-Majorovas, Cannes 1992, showed. A better try is 14...♘d4 although the old game Tolush-Szabo, Bucharest 1953, was

a disaster for Black: 15 ♗e4 ♘df5 16 ♗xf5 exf5 17 ♘b5 0-0 18 ♕e2 ♘g6 19 ♗xf8 ♘xf8 20 ♘c7 ♖b8 21 ♘e8. The move 13...♕a5+ is new and probably better than 13...♕f6. Black's queen takes up an active position and keeps the knight on c3 under control.

14 ♘c3   ♘f5
15 ♗e4

In this position 15 ♗xc6+?! is harmless.

15 ...   ♗d7
16 ♗xf5   exf5

It is important to keep the queen on a5. After 16...♕xf5 White has an immediately winning continuation with 17 ♘b5 0-0-0 18 ♗g3 ♕e4+ 19 ♕e2 ♕xe2+ 20 ♔xe2 and Black cannot prevent the destructive 21 ♘d6+.

17 ♕e2+   ♗e6
18 0-0-0   0-0-0
19 ♖xg7

White has regained his pawn and has the better pawn structure, but in the meantime Black has completed his development and now starts a counterattack.

19 ...   ♕a6! *(D)*

Again a major role for the queen. White cannot defend the pawn with 20 b3 because of 20...♖xd6! However, he can draw by perpetual check with the elegant 20 ♘b5 ♕xa2 21 ♕xe6+! fxe6 22 ♖c7+. Instead the Icelandic grandmaster chooses a safe continuation which drops a pawn but immediately results in an endgame with opposite-coloured bishops.

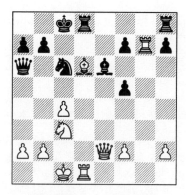

20	**c5!?**		**♕xe2**
21	**♘xe2**		**♗xa2**
22	**♘d4**		**♘xd4**
23	**♖xd4**		**♗e6**

The alternative 23...♖dg8 might lead to a slight edge for Black after 24 ♖xg8+ ♖g8 25 ♖a4 ♗d5 26 ♖xa7 ♖g2 27 ♖a8+ ♔d7 28 ♖h8 ♖xf2 29 ♖xh7 f4! However, White can easily equalize with 27 ♗g3.

24	**♖h4**		**h6**
25	**♖g3**		**♖dg8**
26	**♖xh6**		**♖xh6**
27	**♖xg8+**		**♔d7**
28	**♖a8**		**a6**
29	**♖b8**		**♔c6**
30	**♖e8**		**b6!?**

This move leads to some final tactical complications, but the position remains balanced.

31	**cxb6**		**♗d7**
32	**♗f4**		**♖h4**
33	**b7**		**♔xb7**
34	**♖e7**		**♖xf4**
35	**♖xd7+**		**♔c6**
36	**♖d2**		**♖f3**
37	**♔d1**		**♖h3**
38	**♖c2+**		**♔d5**
39	**♖c7**		**♖xh2**
40	**♔e2**		**♖h6**
41	**♖xf7**		**♔e5**
42	**♖e7+**		**♔f4**
43	**♖e3**		**♖b6**
44	**♖f3+**		**½-½**

Game 38
I.Sokolov – San Segundo
Madrid 1994

1	**d4**		**d5**
2	**c4**		**c6**
3	**♘c3**		**e6**
4	**e4**		**dxe4**
5	**♘xe4**		**♗b4+**
6	**♗d2**		**♕xd4**
7	**♗xb4**		**♕xe4+**
8	**♗e2**		**c5**
9	**♗c3!?**		**♘e7**

Now 9...♕xg2? is not such a good idea. After 10 ♗f3 ♕g5 11 ♘e2 followed by 12 ♖g1 or 12 ♕d6

White has tremendous compensation. Careful players might choose 9...f6 10 ♘f3 ♕f4 11 0-0 ♘e7! (11...♘c6?! 12 ♘d2! ♘ge7 13 ♗h5+ ♘g6 14 g3 ♕c7 15 ♘e4 0-0 16 ♘xc5 ♘ce5!? leads to an unclear position with approximately equal chances, Kamsky-Kramnik, New York match 1994) 12 ♗d3 (12 b4 ♘a6 13 bxc5 ♘xc5 14 ♘d4 ♗d7 is slightly better for Black) 12...♘bc6 13 ♖e1 and now 13...0-0 leads to the text game. Instead Tempone-Slipak, Buenos Aires 1995, went 13...♗d7 14 a3 0-0-0 15 b4 ♘d4 16 ♗xd4 cxd4 17 b5 ♔b8 18 c5 and White's attack looked impressive although Black eventually won the game.

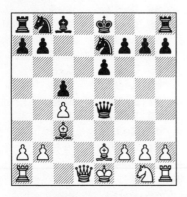

10 ♘f3
10 ♗xg7 leads to a slight advantage for Black after 10...♖g8 11 ♗f6 ♘d7 12 ♗xe7 ♔xe7.
10 ...   0-0
11 0-0
In the game Vladimirov-Stoliar, Leningrad 1955, 11 ♕d2 ♘g6 12 0-0 ♕f4 13 ♕c2 ♘c6 14 ♗d2 ♕c7

15 ♗e3 b6 gave Black better prospects.
11 ...   f6?!
More to the point is 11...♘bc6 intending ...♖d8 or ...e5.
12 ♗d3   ♕f4
13 ♖e1   ♘bc6
14 ♘d2   ♖d8
A more solid alternative is 14...e5 15 ♘e4 ♗f5 (15...b6!? looks risky but possible) 16 ♘xc5 ♖ad8 (better is 16...♖fd8!? e.g. 17 ♘e4 ♘d4) 17 ♘e4 ♖d7 18 ♘c5 ♖d6 (18...♖fd8? 19 ♘xd7 ♖xd7 20 ♗xf5 ♖xd1 21 ♗e6+ and White has more than enough material for the queen) 19 ♘e4 ♖d7 with a draw by repetition.

15 ♘e4

15 ...   f5!
Black has to be careful. 15...♘e5? fails to 16 ♘xf6+! gxf6 17 ♗xe5 fxe5 18 ♗xh7+.
16 g3!
16 ♘xc5? ♕d6 drops a piece.
16 ...   ♕c7!?
After 16...♕h6 17 ♘xc5 White would have had a slight edge, but

the queen sacrifice, 16...♕xe4! 17 ♖xe4 fxe4, would have given Black the better prospects, though White has some counterplay after 18 ♗xg7! ♖xd3 19 ♕g4 e5 20 ♕g5 ♘g6. Now White starts a kingside attack which looks dangerous.

17 ♘g5   e5

17...h6 18 ♘xe6 ♗xe6 19 ♖xe6 ♕d7 20 ♖e3 is better for White.

18 ♕h5!   h6
19 ♕f7+   ♔h8
20 ♘f3

White has tremendous pressure on e5, but Black finds a solution. Note that 20...♖xd3? is impossible because of 21 ♘xe5 ♖xc3 22 ♘xc6 ♕xc6 23 ♖xe7.

20 ...   ♘d5!
21 ♘g5

The only way to keep the attack going. After 21 ♕xc7?! ♘xc7 22 ♘xe5 ♘xe5 23 ♗xe5 ♖xd3 24 ♗xc7 ♗d7 the endgame is about equal.

21 ...   ♘de7

After 21...hxg5 22 ♕h5+ ♔g8 23 cxd5 White has a large advantage.

22 h4?! *(D)*

White plays for more than a draw and bluffs his way to victory.

22 ...   hxg5?

Black cannot be greedy in this position. Both the text move and 22...♖xd3? 23 ♗xe5 ♘xe5 24 ♖xe5 ♕xe5 25 ♕f8+ ♘g8 26 ♘f7+ lose in straightforward fashion. However, Black could have successfully defended his position with 22...♗d7! After 23 ♘f3 ♖f8 the attack is over, 23 ♘e6 ♗xe6 24 ♕xe6

♖xd3 loses a piece and though the sacrifice 23 ♖xe5 ♘xe5 24 ♕xe7 ♖e8 25 ♘f7+ looks winning after the continuation 25...♘xf7 26 ♕xf7 ♖g8 27 ♗xf5 ♖ad8 28 ♕g6, the calm move 25...♔g8 is a sufficient defence.

23 hxg5   ♗e6

There is no other defence against ♔g2 and ♖h1, for example 23...♘d4 24 ♔g2 ♕c6+ 25 ♗e4 or 23...f4 24 ♗e4. However, 23...♗e6 is also insufficient and Sokolov must have enjoyed the rest of the game.

24	**♕xe6**	**♘d4**
25	**♗xd4**	**♖xd4**
26	**♗xf5**	**♘xf5**
27	**♕xf5**	**♖e8**
28	**g6**	**♔g8**
29	**♕h5**	**♖e6**
30	**♕h7+**	**♔f8**
31	**♕h8+**	**♔e7**
32	**♕xg7+**	**♔d6**
33	**♕f8+**	**♕e7**
34	**g7**	**1-0**

Instead of the normal 8 ♗e2, White can also play the equally interesting 8 ♘e2.

Game 39
Tunik – Sveshnikov
St Petersburg 1994

1 d4	d5
2 c4	e6
3 ♘c3	c6
4 e4	dxe4
5 ♘xe4	♗b4+
6 ♗d2	♕xd4
7 ♗xb4	♕xe4+
8 ♘e2	♘a6 *(D)*

Also playable is 8...♘d7!? (the line 8...♘e7 9 ♕d2! c5 10 0-0-0 0-0 11 ♗xc5 leads to a favourable position for White, G.Georgadze-Cruz Lopez, San Sebastian 1991), when after 9 ♕d6 Black has two solid options:

- 9...a5!? 10 ♗c3 (alternatively 10 ♗a3 e5! with a slight edge for Black) 10...♘gf6 (the position is unclear after 10...♘e7!? 11 0-0-0 e5 12 ♘g3 ♕f4 13 ♗d2 ♕xf2 14 ♘e4 ♕f5 15 ♗d3) 11 b3 c5 12 ♖d1 ♖a6 with a level position in the game Grigore-Cozianu, Romania championship 1993.
- 9...e5 10 0-0-0 c5! 11 ♗c3 (not 11 ♗xc5?? ♕xc4+) 11...♘e7 12 ♘g3 ♕f4+ 13 ♖d2 a5 with equal chances in P.Nikolić-Sveshnikov, Ljubljana 1995.

9 ♗f8!

This remarkable move is White's best choice. After 9 ♗a3 ♗d7 10 ♕d6 0-0-0! 11 0-0-0 e5 Black is out of trouble and still a pawn up, while in the game Malaniuk-Kharlov, Moscow 1992, Black had a

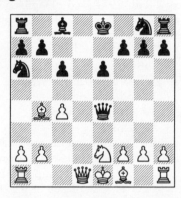

slight advantage after 9 ♗c3 e5 10 ♕d6 f6 11 ♖d1 ♔f7 12 f4 exf4 13 ♖d4 ♕e7 14 ♕xf4 ♘h6.

9 ...   ♘e7

Black tried 9...♗d7!? with the intention 10 ♗xg7 ♘b4 in the game Schwartzman-Komarov, Metz. After 10 ♕d6 0-0-0 11 ♗xg7 ♗e8 12 ♕a3 ♖d3 13 b3 c5 14 f3! ♕h4+ 15 ♘g3 ♕g5 16 ♗xd3 ♕xg7 17 0-0! White won in convincing fashion.

10 ♗xg7   ♖g8

The sacrifice 10...♘b4 used to be the normal move in this position. After 11 ♗xh8 e5 12 ♕d6 ♘c2+ 13 ♔d2 ♗f5 White's best option 14 ♖d1!? ♖d8 15 ♕xd8+ ♔xd8 16 ♔c1+ ♔e8 17 ♘c3 ♕f4+ 18 ♖d2 is merely sufficient for a tiny edge. The same evaluation is applicable after 11 ♕d6 ♘d3+ 12 ♔d2 ♘f5 13 ♕xd3 ♕xd3 14 ♔xd3 ♘xg7 Vaiser-Flear, San Sebastian 1992.

11 ♗f6

White has two alternatives:
- 11 ♗c3!? ♕xc4 (both 11...♘c5 12 ♕d4 and 11...e5 12 ♕d6 ♗f5 13 ♖d1! are better for White) 12 ♘g3 ♕d5 13 ♕c2 with some compensation.
- 11 ♕d4 ♕xd4 12 ♗xd4 c5 13 ♗c3 ♘c6!? 14 0-0-0 e5 15 ♘g3 ♗e6 16 ♗d3 h6 17 ♗e4 ♘ab4 18 ♗xb4 cxb4 with equality, P.Nik-olić-Lautier, Monaco 1996.

11	...	♖g6
12	♕d4	♕xd4
13	♗xd4	c5
14	♗c3	♘b4

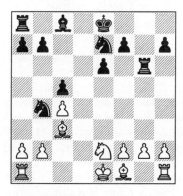

15 ♔d2?!
Very risky. A safe road to an equal position is 15 ♘f4 ♘c2+ 16 ♔d2 ♘xa1 17 ♘xg6 or 15 ♗xb4 cxb4 16 ♘d4. Now Black plays a promising pawn sacrifice.

15	...	e5!
16	♗xe5	♘ec6
17	♗g3	

Black is better after 17 ♗c3 ♖d6+ or 17 f4 ♗f5!

| 17 | ... | ♗f5 |
| 18 | ♘f4 | 0-0-0+ |

| 19 | ♔c3 | ♖gd6 |
| 20 | a3 | |

The variation 20 ♘d5 ♖xd5 21 cxd5 ♘xd5+ 22 ♔c4 ♘b6+ 23 ♔b5 c4 24 ♗xc4 ♗d3! 25 ♗xd3 ♖d5 checkmate shows how dangerous White's situation is.

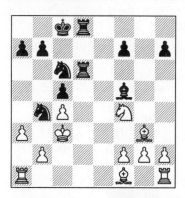

| 20 | ... | ♖d2! |

Black must go for it as 20...♘a6 21 ♘d5 is perfect for White.

21	axb4	cxb4+
22	♔b3	♗c2+
23	♔a2	♘d4

Not 23...♘a5? 24 ♖c1 ♖d1 25 ♗e2! and White is winning.

24 ♗d3?
The only move is 24 ♖e1, after which Black should force a draw with 24...♗b3+ 25 ♔b1 ♗c2+ 26 ♔a2. In this position 26...♖d6 27 c5 ♖c6 28 ♘h5! is sufficient for White, though Black can still make a draw with 28...♗b3+.

24	...	b3+
25	♔a3	♗xd3
26	♖ac1	

Black also has a huge advantage after 26 ♖ad1 ♘c2+ 27 ♔a4 ♗xc4!

26 ...   &c2!
27 &he1
Or 27 &b4 &c6+ 28 &c3 &8d3+
29 &xd3 &xd3 checkmate!
27 ...   &c6
28 &e2
Again 28 &d5 &8xd5 29 cxd5
&xd5 30 &xc2 bxc2 is better for
Black.

28 ...   a6
29 &f4   &2d3
30 &e3
White is lost as 30 &c3 fails to
30...b5 31 cxb5 axb5 32 &xb5 &b7.

30 ...   b5
31 &f4   &3d7
32 cxb5   axb5 *(D)*
In order to save his king White
must now part with his rook on c1.

33 &xc2   bxc2
34 &c1   &d4!
35 b3
Or 35 &xd4 &xd4 36 &xc2+
&b7 with the same result: Black
wins the endgame.

35 ...   &c7
36 &b2   &b7
37 g3   &c6
38 &xd4   &xd4
39 &xc2   &cd6!

It is easier with two rooks.

40 &e2   b4
41 &c2   &c8
42 &g2   &a6
43 &b2   &d1
44 &e1   &da1
45 &c2   &1a2+
          0-1

If Black wishes to avoid the ad-
ventures of the previous games, he
has a solid alternative in 4...&b4,
declining the gambit. This approach is fairly new, but Black's
results have been promising. The
following game is a typical example: White tries to create tension,
but Black is well prepared.

Game 40
C.Hansen – Maksimenko
Copenhagen 1995

1 c4   e6
2 &c3   d5
3 d4   c6
4 e4   &b4 *(D)*
5 a3

White has several alternatives
none of which gives any advantage:
● 5 &d3 dxe4 6 &xe4 &f6 7 &f3
0-0 8 &e2 &bd7 with equality.

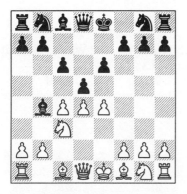

- 5 cxd5 exd5 6 e5 c5 7 a3 &a5 8 ∅f3 ∅c6 9 &b5 ∅e7 10 0-0 cxd4 11 ∅xd4 0-0 with equal chances.
- 5 exd5 exd5 6 cxd5 ♕xd5 7 ∅f3 ∅f6 8 &d3 0-0 9 0-0 ♕a5 (or 9...&xc3 10 bxc3 &g4 11 ♖b1 b5 12 a4 a6 13 axb5 axb5 Petrakov-Skomorokhin, Kstovo 1994, with equality) 10 ♕c2 h6 11 ♖e1 &e6 12 ♖e5 ♕d8 Berg-Schandorff, Ringsted 1995, again with an equal position.
- 5 e5 c5 6 a3 &xc3+ 7 bxc3 ∅e7 8 ∅f3 ∅bc6 9 &d3 (or 9 &e2 cxd4 10 cxd4 b6 11 0-0 &a6 12 cxd5 &xe2 13 ♕xe2 ♕xd5 14 ♖d1 0-0 15 ♖b1 ♖ac8 16 ♖b5 ♕d7 17 ♖b3 ∅a5 with a better position for Black in the game Baburin-S.Ivanov, Kstovo 1994) 9...cxd4 10 cxd4 b6 11 cxd5 ♕xd5 12 0-0 &b7 13 &b2 ∅f5 14 ♖e1 ∅ce7 15 &e4 ♕d7 16 g4 &xe4 17 ♖xe4 ∅h6 18 ♕d3 ∅d5 19 &c1 ∅g8 20 ♖e1 ∅ge7 21 ∅g5 ∅g6 22 ∅e4 0-0 with equal chances in Shirov-Liiva, Tallinn 1996.

5 ...	&xc3+
6 bxc3	dxe4

7 ♕g4	∅f6
8 ♕xg7	♖g8
9 ♕h6	♖g6

Other options are 9...∅bd7 or immediately 9...c5.

10 ♕e3	c5
11 ∅e2	∅c6
12 dxc5!?	

The only move to complete his development, as 12 &d2 ♕a5 does not help White's cause.

12 ...	e5
13 ∅g3	♕a5
14 &e2	∅d4!

15 ♖a2?

Now White gets into trouble. An unclear position arises after the continuation 15 &d1! ∅f5 16 ∅xf5 &xf5, but White's chances are more concrete.

15 ...	∅xe2
16 ♖xe2	&e6
17 0-0	

White has to castle as 17 ∅xe4 ∅xe4 18 ♕xe4 fails to 18...♕xc3+.

17 ...	&xc4
18 ∅xe4	∅xe4
19 ♕xe4	&xe2

20	♕xe5+	♖e6
21	♕h8+	♚d7
22	♕xa8	♕a6!

Black's two threats 23...♖e8 and 23...♗xf1 are too much for White.

23	♕f8	♗xf1

Black correctly judges that his king can evade the white checks.

24	♕xf7+	♖e7
25	♕d5+	♚c8
26	♕f5+	♖d7

27	♗g5

After 27 ♕f8+ ♖d8 28 ♕f5+ ♚b8 29 ♗f4+ ♚a8 White runs out of checks.

27	...	♕a4!

This move combines defence and attack.

28	♕f8+	♚c7
29	♕f4+	

Or 29 ♗f4+ ♚c6 30 ♕c8+ ♚d5 and Black's advantage is decisive.

29	...	♕xf4
30	♗xf4+	♚c6
31	♚xf1	a5!

31...♚c5 32 ♗e3+ ♚c4 33 ♗xa7 would have ruined everything. Now with the a-pawn on the board Black has an easy endgame.

32 ♗e3 ♖d1+ 33 ♚e2 ♖a1 34 ♚d3 ♖xa3 35 g4 ♖a1 36 h4 a4 37 ♚c2 ♖g1 38 g5 ♖h1 39 f4 ♖xh4 40 f5 ♚d5 41 ♚b2 ♖h3 42 ♗d4 ♖g3 43 g6 hxg6 44 f6 ♚c4 45 ♚a3 ♚b5 0-1

10 Anti-Noteboom systems: Exchange variation

White's second favourite way to avoid the Noteboom variation, after the Marshall Gambit, is to opt for a kind of Exchange variation of the Queen's Gambit with 1 d4 d5 2 c4 e6 3 ♘c3 c6 4 cxd5 exd5. The major difference from the Queen's Gambit is that Black has played ...c6 instead of ...♘f6 so White's queen's bishop is usually committed to f4 rather than g5. This is clearly in Black's favour because he will generally be able to play ...♗f5 very quickly, solving the problem of the development of his light-squared bishop. A common motif in all variations here is that

if White prepares queenside expansion with b2-b4, Black will play ...a7-a5 to slow him down.

Although Black can reach equality quite easily, it is much more difficult to play for a win in these positions, even against lower-rated opponents. However, new methods based on answering ♗f4 with a timely ...♕b6, especially if White has already played ♘f3, have somewhat changed this view (see game 42).

White has two major continuations on his fifth move: 5 ♗f4 and 5 ♘f3, which are discussed in games 41 and 42 respectively.

Game 41
Spassky – Dorfman
France team tournament 1993

1	d4	d5
2	c4	e6
3	♘c3	c6
4	cxd5	exd5
5	♗f4	

In this game we only deal with continuations in which White does not play ♘f3 or plays it at a late moment. Otherwise play will transpose to game 42. White sometimes plays 5 ♕c2 in order to prevent ...♗f5, but after 5...♗d6 (5...g6,

preparing ...♗f5, is an interesting alternative) 6 ♘f3 ♘e7 7 ♗g5 ♗g4 8 e3 ♗h5 9 ♗d3 ♗g6 10 0-0 ♘a6 11 a3 ♘c7 12 b4 0-0 Black had at least equal chances in Bener-Lau, Ostend open 1993.

| 5 | ... | ♗f5 |

Black's safest continuation is 5...♗d6 to exchange dark-squared bishops. This exchange is often followed by the same fate for their light-squared counterparts, after which a very equal position arises. Usually the game transposes into the note 6...♗d6 in game 42, e.g. 6 ♗xd6 ♕xd6 7 e3 ♗f5 8 ♘f3. An independent line is 6 ♗g3 ♘e7!? (6...♗f5 7 ♘f3 ♘f6 also transposes) 7 e3 ♘f5 8 ♗d3 ♘xg3 9 hxg3 ♘d7 10 ♘ge2 ♘f6 11 ♕c2 ♕e7 12 ♗f5 ♗xf5 13 ♕xf5 g6 14 ♕d3 ♘g4 and an equal position resulted in the game M.Muse-Stangl, Bundesliga 1995.

The active 5...♕b6 6 ♕d2 ♘f6 7 e3 ♗f5 8 f3 will transpose to the note 6...♕b6 below, and 8 ♘ge2 to the note 7 ♘ge2 in the game.

The position after the less active 5...♗e7 is most likely to come from the 3 ♘c3 ♗e7 4 cxd5 exd5 5 ♗f4 c6 move order. A well-known example is Kasparov-Karpov, Moscow (game 21) 1985, which went 6 e3 ♗f5 7 g4 ♗e6 8 h4 ♘d7 9 h5 ♘h6!? 10 ♗e2 ♘b6 11 ♖c1 ♗d6?! (better is 11...♘c4) 12 ♘h3 ♗xf4 13 ♘xf4 ♗d7 14 ♖g1! and White had an edge.

6 e3　　　　　♘f6

Here 6...♕b6 is also possible. The game Tondivar-Kharlov, Leeuwarden 1993, continued 7 ♕d2 (unnecessarily passive is 7 ♕c1?! ♘f6 8 ♘f3 ♗e7 9 ♗e2 ♘bd7 10 h3 0-0 11 0-0 ♖e8 12 a3 a5 with a small plus for Black in Soman-Novikov, Calcutta 1996) 7...♘f6 8 f3 ♘bd7 (8...h5!?, preventing White's plans on the kingside, is an interesting idea, for example 9 0-0-0 ♘a6 10 ♗d3 ♗xd3 11 ♕xd3 ♗e7 12 ♘h3 ♘b4 13 ♕d2 0-0-0

with an equal position in Budde-Flear, Bundesliga 1983) 9 g4 ♗e6 10 ♘ge2 h5 11 g5 ♘g8 12 h4 ♘ge7 with a complex position. White has a small advantage, but Black is not without counterplay.

7 ♗d3

Alternatives are 7 ♘f3 ♕b6!, transposing to game 42, and 7 ♘ge2 and then:

- 7...♗d6 8 ♗xd6 ♕xd6 9 ♘g3 ♗g6 10 h4 h6?! (now the f5 square becomes weak, so 10...h5 was preferable) 11 h5 ♗h7 12 ♗d3 ♗xd3 13 ♕xd3 0-0 14 0-0-0 ♘bd7 15 ♔b1 with an edge for White in Terterians-Kharlov, Podolsk team tournament 1992. After 15...♕e6?! 16 ♘ce2 ♘b6 17 ♘f4 ♕d7 18 f3 a5 19 ♘f5 a4 20 ♖h3 ♔h8 21 ♖g3 ♘e8 22 e4 White had a strong attack.

- 7...♕b6 8 ♕d2 ♘bd7 9 ♘g3 ♗g6 10 ♗d3 c5!? 11 0-0 c4 12 ♗xg6 hxg6 13 b3 and White was a little better in the game Velikov-Kupreichik, Frunze 1985.

7 ...　　　　　♗xd3
8 ♕xd3　　　　♘bd7

Again 8...♗d6 is the safe continuation, e.g. 9 ♗xd6 ♕xd6 10 ♘f3 or 9 ♗g3 0-0 10 ♘f3 with transposition to the note 6...♗d6 in game 42.

9 h3　　　　　♗e7
10 ♘ge2　　　0-0
11 0-0　　　　♖e8
12 ♖ad1　　　♘b6
13 b3　　　　♘h5

Black would like to exchange off White's bishop on f4, but the immediate 13...♗d6 would be met by 14 ♗g5.

14	♗h2	♗d6
15	♗xd6	♕xd6
16	g4!?	

White expands his territory on the kingside, at a moment when Black has no way to exploit the weaknesses that are created by the pawn moves.

16	...	♘f6
17	f3	♕e7
18	♔f2	♘fd7?!

This plan is too slow. It will take a lot of time for the knight on b6 to participate in the battle in the centre and on the kingside.

| 19 | ♘g3 | g6 |

Black cannot allow a white knight on f5.

| 20 | ♖fe1 | ♖ad8 |
| 21 | ♘ce2! | ♘a8! |

Both players are optimizing the position of their knights.

22	♘f4	♘c7
23	♔g2	♘e6
24	♘xe6	♕xe6
25	h4!	

| 25 | ... | ♕e7 |
| 26 | g5 | |

With his last two moves Spassky fixes the weak dark squares on Black's kingside. Dorfman's next move aims at opening the h-file, but White is the only one to profit from it.

26	...	h6?!
27	f4	hxg5
28	hxg5	♔g7
29	e4!	dxe4
30	♘xe4	♕b4
31	♖h1	♕b5

The alternatives 31...♕a5 32 d5 and 31...♖h8 32 f5! gxf5 33 ♘g3 are no better.

32	♕xb5	cxb5
33	♔f3	♖h8
34	d5	♖xh1
35	♖xh1 (D)	

In this endgame White has very good winning chances due to his active pieces and passed d-pawn.

35	...	♖c8
36	d6	b4
37	♔e3	♖c6
38	♖h2	a5
39	♖d2	♔f8

40	Rh2	Kg7
41	f5! (D)	

Spassky plays as if in his second youth, combining tactics and strategy. Due to the threat of 42 f6+, Black has no other choice but to take on f5, thereby further weakening his position.

41	...	gxf5
42	Ng3	Rc1
43	Kf4!	Kg8
44	Re2	Kf8
45	Re7	Nc5

46 Kxf5

Now that the white rook has entered the position, Black has no defence.

The remaining moves of the game were:

46...Rg1 47 Rc7 Rxg3 48 Rc8+ Kg7 49 Rxc5 Rd3 50 Ke5 Re3+ 51 Kd4 Re1 52 Rxa5 Rd1+ 53 Kc5 Kg6 54 Rb5 Kxg5 55 Rxb4 f5 56 Rxb7 Kf6 57 Rb6 Rc1+ 58 Kd5 Re1 59 Kc6 Rc1+ 60 Kd7 Rh1 61 Rb4 Ke5 62 Kc7 1-0

Game 42
P.Claesen – Korchnoi
Antwerp open 1995

1	c4	e6
2	Nc3	d5
3	cxd5	exd5
4	d4	c6
5	Nf3	Bf5
6	Bf4	

An important alternative here is 6 Bg5, when Black can choose between the solid 6...Be7 7 Bxe7 Wxe7! (now the king's knight can

develop to the natural f6 square) 8 e3 Nf6 9 Bd3 Bxd3 10 Wxd3 Nbd7 11 0-0 0-0 12 Rc1 Ne4 and Black has no problems, Porper-Shvidler, Ramat Gan 1992 or 6...Wb6 (the most active reply) 7 Wd2 Nd7 8 e3 (8 We3+?! Be6 9 0-0-0 h6 10 Bh4 Nf6 11 h3 Bb4 12 Ne5 0-0 and Black was already slightly better in Deak-L.Portisch,

Hungary 1994) 8...♘gf6 (8...h6 9 ♗h4 ♘gf6 seems even more accurate, because ...h7-h6 is often a useful move) 9 ♗xf6 ♘xf6 10 ♘h4 ♘e4! 11 ♕c2 ♗e6 12 f4 (or 12 ♗d3 ♗e7 13 ♘f3 f5 with equal prospects) 12...f5 13 ♘f3 h6 and Black had a fine position in Huss-Klinger, San Bernardino 1988.

Other moves that have been played here are:

• 6 ♕b3 ♕b6! 7 ♕xb6 (7 ♘a4 ♕xb3 8 axb3 ♘a6 9 ♗d2 ♘f6 10 e3 ♘b4 with equality in Onischuk-Sherbakov, Berlin open 1993) 7...axb6 8 ♗f4 ♘f6 9 e3 b5 and Black already had an edge in the game Lampen-Sherbakov, Jyvaskyla open 1994.

• 6 e3 ♗d6 7 ♗d3 ♗xd3 8 ♕xd3 ♘f6 9 0-0 0-0 10 e4 dxe4 11 ♘xe4 ♘xe4 12 ♕xe4 ♖e8 13 ♕d3 ♘d7 and Black was at least equal in Ghijsen-Van der Vorm, Sassenheim 1994.

• 6 g3 ♗e7 7 ♗g2 ♘d7 8 0-0 h6 9 h3 ♘gf6 10 ♗f4 0-0 11 ♘e5 ♗h7 12 g4 ♕b6 13 ♘a4 ♕b5 14 ♘xd7 ♘xd7 15 b3 ♖ae8 and Black had equalized in Miladinović-Ivanchuk, Belgrade 1995.

6 ... ♕b6!?

The best move order is probably 6...♘f6 7 e3 ♕b6!, because here 8 ♘a4 makes no sense. As a rule of thumb ...♕b6 is most effective after White has played ♘f3, so that f2-f3 is not possible in the short term. Sriram-Novikov, Calcutta open 1996, continued 8 ♕c1 (8 ♕d2 is answered by 8...♘e4 9 ♘xe4??

dxe4 10 ♘e5 ♗b4 winning the queen) 8...♘bd7 9 ♗e2 ♗e7 10 0-0 0-0 11 h3 ♖e8 12 a3 a5 with a good game for Black.

Also possible is the safe continuation 6...♗d6:

• 7 ♗xd6 ♕xd6 8 e3 ♘f6 9 ♗d3 ♗xd3 10 ♕xd3 0-0 11 h3 (after 11 0-0 ♘bd7 Balashov-Sveshnikov, Vladivostok open 1994 was agreed drawn) 11...♘bd7 12 0-0 ♖e8 13 ♘d2 ♘f8 14 ♖b1 a5 15 a3 a4 16 ♕c2 b5 and Black developed an initiative on the queenside in Scekić-Novoselski, Cetinje 1993.

• 7 ♗g3 ♘f6 8 e3 0-0 9 ♗d3 (9 ♘h4 ♗e4 10 f3 ♗g6 11 ♘xg6 hxg6 12 ♕d2 ♖e8 did not trouble Black in Savon-I.Novikov, Belgorod 1991) 9...♗xd3 10 ♕xd3 ♖e8 11 ♘e2 (11 0-0 ♘e4 12 ♗xd6 ♕xd6 13 ♘e5 ♘bd7 14 ♘xd7 ♕xd7 led to equality in the game Sutmuller-Van der Vorm, Eindhoven 1994) 11...♕e7 12 0-0 ♘bd7 13 ♖b1 a5 with an equal position in Sorin-I.Novikov, Alicante open 1992.

7 ♘a4

7 ♕c1 ♗e7 8 e3 ♘d7 9 ♗e2 ♘gf6 10 0-0 0-0 11 h3 ♖e8 (Robert-G.Flear, Bern open 1993) and 7 ♕b3 ♘f6 8 e3 ♗e7 9 ♗e2 ♘bd7 10 ♘d2 0-0 11 0-0 ♖e8 12 ♖c1 ♗g6 13 h3 ♘f8 (Jostes-Rausis, Gausdal open 1995) do not promise White anything.

7 ... ♕a5+
8 ♗d2 ♕c7
9 b4

In the next round of the Antwerp open the game Abolianin-Van der Vorm featured 9 ♖c1 ♘f6 10 ♕b3 ♗e7! (Black has no fear of White's plan to exchange the dark-squared bishops via b4, because he gains some tempi compared to lines where the bishops are exchanged with ♗c1-♗f4xd6) 11 ♗b4 0-0 12 ♗xe7 ♕xe7 13 e3 ♘bd7! 14 ♗e2 ♖ab8 15 0-0 ♘e4 16 ♖fd1 ♖fe8 17 ♘e1 ♕h4 (Black suddenly switches to the kingside) 18 g3 ♕g5 19 ♘g2 ♖e6 20 f4?! ♕h6 21 g4?! (21 ♘h4 ♕xh4! is a convincing queen sacrifice) 21...♕h3! with a winning attack.

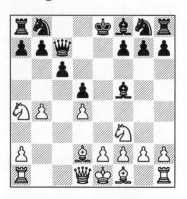

9	...	♘f6
10	e3	♘e4
11	b5	♗a3!?
12	♕b3	♕e7
13	bxc6	bxc6
14	♗d3	♘d7
15	♖b1	

Black has a dangerous initiative after the continuation 15 ♕b7 ♖b8 16 ♕xc6 ♗b4.

| 15 | ... | a5 |

Preventing the exchange of bishops with 16 ♗b4. Now after 16 ♕b7 0-0 17 ♕xc6 ♘xd2 18 ♗xf5 ♘xb1 19 ♗xb1 ♖ac8 Black wins.

16	♕c2	0-0
17	0-0	

17 ♕xc6 leads to the previous note.

| 17 | ... | ♗g4! |

Again preventing ♕xc6 by tactical means.

18	♗c1	♗d6
19	♘d2	f5
20	♕xc6!	

At the right moment White takes up the challenge.

20	...	♕e6
21	♗b5	♘df6
22	♘b6	♖ab8
23	f4	♗h5!

Threatening 24...♗e8.

24	♘xe4	♕xe4
25	♖b3	

25 ♗d2 is strongly answered by 25...♗xf4!

| 25 | ... | ♕e6 |

Again threatening 26...♗e8.

| 26 | ♘c4!? | |

28	Rb3	Rxb5
29	Rxb5	dxc4
30	Re5	Wd7
31	Wxc4+?	

After 31 Wxd7 ♘xd7 32 Rd5 Rf6 33 Ra5 ♗e2 34 Re1 ♗d3 35 ♗xa3 Black must still work to win.

| 31 | ... | ♗f7 |

White must have totally overlooked this move.

32	Wd3	♗xe5
33	fxe5	♘e4
34	♗xa3	Rc8

0-1

26	...	a4!
27	Rb2	a3

11 Anti-Noteboom systems: Other setups

This chapter discusses some unusual systems that white players have tried to avoid the Noteboom; they all arise after the moves 1 d4 d5 2 c4 e6. Game 43 deals with the system 3 ♘c3 c6 4 ♗f4 in which the bishop on f4 prevents Black from playing a real Noteboom setup. In game 44 (3 ♘c3 c6 4 e3) and game 45 (3 ♘f3 c6 4 e3) White blocks his dark-squared bishop to defend c4 immediately. This system has always been quite a popular way to avoid the mass of Noteboom and Marshall Gambit theory, and at the same time avoid the equalizing Exchange variation. Finally games 46 and 47 deal with the positional setup 3 ♘f3 c6 4 ♕c2.

Game 43
Finegold – Bagirov
Amsterdam open 1989

1	d4	d5
2	c4	e6
3	♘c3	c6
4	♗f4	dxc4!

This is the most Noteboom-like way to play. After 4...♘f6 5 e3 ♘bd7 6 ♘f3 ♗e7 Black has a very passive variation of the Queen's Gambit, while 4...♗d6 is too committal: 5 ♗xd6 ♕xd6 6 e4 dxe4 7 c5! ♕e7 8 ♘xe4 ♘f6 9 ♘d6+ and Black had big problems in Miles-Tröger, Porz 1982.

5 e3

Other tries have also failed to prove any advantage:

- 5 e4 b5 6 ♘f3 ♘f6 7 ♕c2 ♗b7 8 ♗e2 ♘bd7 9 0-0 ♗e7 10 ♖fe1 0-0 enabled Black to keep his extra pawn without too much trouble in the game Kneževič-Lukacs, Sarajevo 1981.

- 5 a4 ♗b4 (also playable is 5...♘f6 6 e3 b5 leading to the note 6...♘f6 at Black's sixth move) 6 e3 ♕a5! (6...b5?! leads to the note 6...♗b4 at Black's sixth move) 7 ♕c1 ♘d7 8 ♗xc4 e5 9 ♗g3 ♘gf6 10 ♘f3 exd4 11 exd4 0-0 12 0-0 ♘b6 13 ♗d3 ♗f5 14 ♗xf5 ♕xf5 with equal chances in Pieterse-G.Flear, Ostend open 1987.

5	...	b5
6	a4	♕b6!?

Note that 6...♗b4?!, a common move in the Noteboom, is very risky here. After the continuation 7 axb5 cxb5 8 ♕f3 ♕d5 9 ♕g3

Black is forced into a dubious piece sacrifice with 9...♘e7 10 ♗xb8. Although this line has been seen quite often, Black's results remain disappointing. A solid alternative to the text move is 6...♘f6, for example 7 axb5 cxb5 8 ♘xb5 (8 ♕f3 ♘d5 9 ♗xb8 ♖xb8 10 ♖xa7 ♗e7 is good for Black) 8...♗b4+ 9 ♘c3 ♘d5 10 ♘ge2 ♘c6 11 ♗g3 0-0 12 ♕c2 f5 13 ♖d1 ♕a5 14 ♖c1 ♗a6 15 ♘f4, as in Miles-Ribli, German Bundesliga 1985.

7 ♕f3

7 ♗e2 ♘f6 8 ♗f3 ♗b7 9 a5 ♕a6 10 ♗g5 ♘bd7 11 ♗xf6 ♘xf6 12 ♗e2 ♗b4 proved to be excellent for Black in Ragozin-Sherbakov, St Petersburg 1995.

7 ... ♗b7

7...bxa4!? 8 ♘ge2 ♗b4 9 ♕g3 ♘e7 10 e4 ♘d7 11 ♖xa4 c5 12 f3 0-0 with a complex position was seen in Murey-Sveshnikov, Moscow open 1991.

8 a5 ♕a6

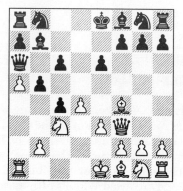

At first sight the queen seems to be out of place on a6, but a timely ...c6-c5 will bring her majesty back into the game. Moreover, the pawn on a5 remains weak.

9	♕g3	♘d7
10	♗e2	♘gf6
11	♘h3	♗b4
12	0-0	0-0
13	♗h6	♘e8
14	♗f4	

Hoping for a draw by repetition of moves, but Black correctly judges that he already stands better.

14 ... c5!

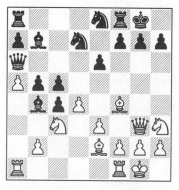

15	♖fd1	♘df6
16	♗f3	♖d8
17	♗e5	cxd4
18	♖xd4	♖xd4
19	exd4	♗xf3
20	♕xf3	♗e7
21	♘g5	h6
22	♘ge4	b4
23	♘e2	♘xe4
24	♕xe4	♘f6
25	♕f3	♘d5
26	♘g3	c3

The alternative is 26...♗f6 27 ♘h5 ♗xe5 28 dxe5 c3 29 bxc3 bxc3 30 ♕g3 g6 and Black's king is quite safe compared to the actual game.

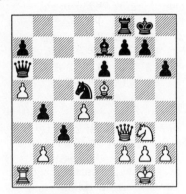

27	bxc3	bxc3
28	♘h5	f6
29	♗f4	♘xf4?!

Bagirov decides to exchange his beautiful knight, due to the threat of 30 ♗xh6. More logical would have been 29...♖f7 30 ♖b1 ♗d6.

30	♘xf4	♖c8
31	♕g4	g5

On 31...c2 White had prepared 32 ♖c1 ♗a3 33 ♘xe6 g5 34 ♘c5 ♗xc5 35 ♖xc2!

32 d5!

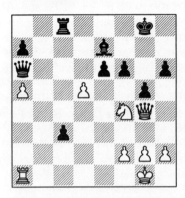

With the idea of 33 dxe6 followed by 34 ♕h5 with a draw by perpetual check.

32	...	♖c4
33	g3	c2
34	♖c1	♕c8

34...e5 35 ♕d7 or 34...exd5 35 ♕d7 ♕d6 36 ♕e8+ ♗f8 37 ♘e6 only puts Black's king in trouble.

35	dxe6	♕c7
36	♕f5	gxf4
37	♕g6+	♔h8

½-½

Game 44
I.Ivanov – Antunes
Thessaloniki olympiad 1988

1	d4	d5
2	c4	e6
3	♘c3	c6
4	e3	f5

This leads to a kind of Stonewall variation of the Dutch Defence with White's bishop inside the pawn chain. Instead Black often plays 4...♘f6 here transposing to the Meran variation of the Semi-Slav Defence after 5 ♘f3 ♘bd7, which falls outside the scope of this book. Another possibility is 4...♘d7 to avoid White's fifth move alternatives 5 g4 and 5 f4, but it is not always good to develop the queen's knight to d7 too early in the game, since it hinders the manoeuvre ...♗c8-d7-e8.

5 ♘f3

White has a number of interesting alternatives to the text move. One idea is the gambit 5 g4!? fxg4 (this is the common continuation, but practice suggests that 5...♘f6!? might be better, for example 6 gxf5 exf5 7 cxd5 ♘xd5 8 ♗c4 ♗e6 9 ♕b3 ♗b4!? 10 ♘e2 b5 11 ♗xd5 ♗xd5 12 ♕xb4 a5! and in Lalev-Semkov, Bankia Bulgarian championship 1992, White saw nothing better than the hopeless queen sacrifice 13 ♘xd5) 6 ♕xg4 ♘f6 7 ♕g2 c5 and now:

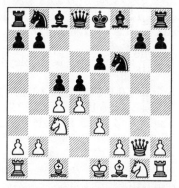

- 8 cxd5 exd5 9 ♗d3 ♘c6 10 ♘ge2 ♗e6 11 dxc5 ♕d7 12 ♘d4 ♗h3 13 ♕g3 ♗xc5 14 ♖g1 ♗xd4 15 exd4 0-0 16 ♗h6 ♖ae8+ 17 ♔d2 ♖f7 with a complex position in Zviaginsev-I.Sokolov, Reykjavik open 1994.
- 8 ♘f3 ♘c6 9 ♗d2 a6?! 10 0-0-0 ♕c7 11 dxc5 ♗xc5 12 ♖g1 0-0 13 ♘g5 ♔h8 14 ♔b1 ♘e5 15 ♘a4

♗a7? 16 ♗b4 ♖g8 17 ♕g3! and Black resigned due to the threat of 18 ♕xe5, Seirawan-Yermolinsky, US championship 1994.

Another idea for White is 5 f4!? (known as the Anti-Stonewall, and regarded by Euwe as one of White's most promising systems) 5...♘f6 6 ♘f3 ♗e7 and now:

- 7 ♗d3 0-0 8 0-0 b6 9 b3 ♗b7 10 ♗b2 ♘e4 11 ♖c1 ♘d7 12 ♕e2 ♖f6 13 ♖c2 ♖h6 14 ♖fc1 with an edge for White in Ivanchuk-Nogueiras, Lucerne world team championship 1993.
- 7 ♗e2 0-0 8 0-0 b6 9 ♕c2 ♗b7 10 cxd5 cxd5 11 ♗d2 ♘c6 12 a3 ♘e4 13 ♖fc1 ♖c8 14 ♕d1 ♕d7 15 ♗e1 ♖c7 16 ♖c2 ♘xc3 17 ♖xc3 ♖fc8 18 ♖ac1 ♗d6 19 ♕a4 ♘b8 20 ♕xd7 ♘xd7 21 ♖xc7 ♖xc7 22 ♖xc7 ♗xc7 with an equal ending in the game Karpov-Ivanchuk, Tilburg 1993.

White's most flexible setup is 5 ♗d3 ♘f6 6 ♘ge2 ♗d6 7 f3 0-0 8 ♕c2, when he has the option to castle kingside or queenside and can then choose to play in the centre or on either flank. For example 8...♘a6 9 a3 ♗d7 10 ♗d2 ♘c7 11 0-0 b6 12 b4 and White had a small advantage in Chekhov-Mukhaev, Moscow open 1995.

5 ...   ♘f6
6 ♗d3   ♗d6
7 ♕c2

7 0-0 0-0 looks like a standard position for this line, as both players have developed to the most natural squares. However, we only

have some 'golden oldies' from this position, and hardly any modern games played by grandmasters. It seems that nowadays White players are very reluctant to play this line because of Black's attacking chances.

- 8 ♘e2 was played in the famous game Glucksberg-Najdorf, Warsaw 1935, which went 8...♘bd7 9 ♘g5 ♗xh2+! 10 ♔h1 ♘g4 11 f4 ♕e8 12 g3 ♕h5 13 ♔g2 ♗g1 14 ♘xg1 ♕h2+ 15 ♔f3 e5! 16 dxe5 ♘dxe5+ 17 fxe5 ♘xe5+ 18 ♔f4 ♘g6+ 19 ♔f3 f4 20 exf4 ♗g4+! 21 ♔xg4 ♘e5+ 22 fxe5 h5 mate.
- Another classic is 8 ♘e5 ♗xe5 9 dxe5 ♘g4 10 f4 d4 11 h3 ♘xe5 12 fxe5 dxc3 13 b3 ♕c7 14 ♗a3 c5 15 ♕e1 ♕xe5 16 ♖c1 ♘c6 17 ♖xc3 ♗d7 and Black was a pawn up in Izbinsky-Chigorin, St Petersburg 1905.
- 8 b3 b6?! (in order to develop the bishop to b7, but it seems that the positional setup chosen by Black in the game does not trouble White; reliable alternatives are 8...♘e4 or 8...♗d7 with the idea of 9...♗e8) 9 ♗b2 ♘e4 10 ♘e5 ♗b7 11 ♘e2 ♘d7 12 ♖c1 ♖c8 13 f3 ♘ef6 14 ♘f4 ♕e7 15 ♕e2 c5 16 ♔h1 ♖c7 17 ♖fe1 g6?! (it was better to play 17...♖fc8 immediately) 18 ♕f2 ♖fc8 19 ♕h4 and White had the better prospects in Murdzia-C.Henriksson, Sas van Gent European junior championship 1992. Now that Black's pieces are optimally

placed it is difficult for him to find a constructive plan.

7 ...   ♘e4

Alternatively, Black may play the immediate 7...0-0 since 8 cxd5 cxd5 9 ♘b5 ♗b4+ 10 ♗d2 ♘c6 11 ♘e5 ♗d7 12 ♘xc6 ♗xd2+ 13 ♕xd2 bxc6 is not really a threat.

8 ♘e5

Other moves have been played here as well:

- 8 ♘d2?! 0-0 9 b3 ♗d7 10 g3 e5! 11 dxe5 ♗xe5 12 ♗b2 ♕f6 13 ♖c1 ♘a6 14 a3 ♘ac5 15 cxd5 ♘xf2! 16 ♔xf2 f4 17 ♘ce4 fxg3++ 18 ♔g2 ♘xe4 19 ♖cf1 ♕f2+! 0-1 Bany-Matlak, Wroclaw Polish championship 1987.
- 8 0-0 0-0 9 ♘d2 ♕h4 10 f4 ♘xd2 (10...♘d7!?) 11 ♗xd2 g6 12 c5 ♗c7 13 b4 with a small plus for White in Burmakin-Goriatschkin, Moscow olympiad 1994.

8	...	♘d7
9	♘xd7	♗xd7
10	0-0	0-0
11	f3	♕h4!
12	f4	

12 g3 fails to 12...♘xg3 13 hxg3 ♗xg3 followed by 14...♖f6 and 15...♖g6 or 15...♖h6, when Black has a decisive attack.

The game continued **12...g5 13 ♘e2 ♔h8 14 ♗d2 ♖g8 15 ♗e1 ♕h6 16 ♗xe4 fxe4 17 ♗g3 g4 18 ♕c3 ♕f6 19 b4 h5 20 c5 ♗c7 21 f5!? ♗xg3 22 ♘xg3 exf5 23 ♘xh5 ♕h4** (Black's attack along the h-file is very strong) **24 ♘g3 ♖g7 25 ♖xf5 ♖h7 26 ♖f4 ♕xh2+ 27 ♔f2 ♖h3 28 ♘e2 ♖f3+! 29 ♔e1 ♕xg2 30 ♔d2 ♔g7 31 ♖g1 ♕f2 32 ♔d1 ♖h8** (the invasion of Black's other rook proves to have a decisive effect) **33 ♖e1 ♖h2 34 ♕a3 ♕xe3 35 ♖xf3 ♕xf3 36 ♕b3 a6 37 ♔d2 g3 38 ♕e3 ♔g6 39 ♖g1 ♗g4 0-1**

If White plays 3 ♘f3 and 4 e3 instead of 3 ♘c3 and 4 e3 he retains the option of exchanging dark-squared bishops with b3 and ♗b2, as occurred in the next game. However, he is no longer able to play the flexible setup with ♕c2, ♗d3, f2-f3 and ♘ge2 and the solid setup with f2-f4

Game 45
Korchnoi – Yusupov
Montpellier candidates 1985

1	d4	d5
2	c4	e6
3	♘f3	c6
4	e3	f5

Again Black can instead play a Meran Defence with 4...♘f6 5 ♘c3 ♘bd7. Some Black players have experimented with 4...♗d6 and 4...♘d7, which often transpose to the text while avoiding 4...f5 5 g4!?.

5 ♗d3

A familiar idea from the variation with ♘c3 instead of ♘f3 is to play 5 g4. After 5...fxg4 6 ♘e5 ♘f6 7 h3 g3 8 f4 c5 9 ♘c3 White had a small plus in the game Rashkovsky-Gofshtein, Aktiubinsk 1985.

5	...	♘f6
6	0-0	♗d6

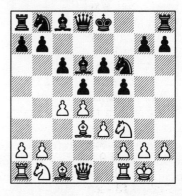

7 b3

Here 7 ♘c3 0-0 would have transposed to the note to White's seventh move in the previous game.

7 ...   ♕e7!?

Forcing White to play 8 a4 before he has the chance for ♗a3, though 7...0-0 is also perfectly playable. Vospernik-Burmakin, Bled open 1995, continued 8 ♗a3 ♗xa3 9 ♘xa3 ♗d7!? 10 b4 ♗e8 11 ♕b3 a6 12 ♘c2 ♘e4 13 ♖fc1 ♘d7 14 ♘ce1?! ♔h8 15 ♕b2 f4! (this illustrates the weaknesses of White's setup; Black's last move is possible because of the exchange of bishops and the fact there is no knight on c3 to control e4) 16 ♗xe4? (16 exf4) 16...dxe4 17 ♘d2 fxe3 18 ♘xe4 ♗g6 19 f3 ♗xe4 20 fxe4 ♕h4 with a very strong Black initiative.

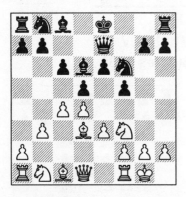

8 a4

Sometimes White refrains from the ♗a3 idea and plays 8 ♗b2, for example 8...0-0 9 ♘e5 ♗d7 10 ♕c1 ♖c8 (better is 10...♗e8) 11 ♘d2 ♘e4 12 f3 ♘xd2 13 ♕xd2 ♗e8 14 e4 and White was a little better in the game Kharitonov-Tregubov, Alusta 1994.

8 ...   0-0

Zsusza Polgar played 8...a5 here in her game against Alisa Marić (Tilburg women candidates 1994).

After 9 ♗a3 ♗xa3 10 ♘xa3 0-0 11 ♕b1 ♘e4! 12 ♕b2 ♘d7 13 ♘c2 b6 14 ♖fc1 ♗b7 15 ♗f1 f4! 16 ♖e1 c5 she assesses the position as unclear.

9 ♗a3   ♗xa3
10 ♘xa3

The other capture 10 ♖xa3 was successful in Gulko-L.Milov, Bern open 1994, after the continuation 10...g6?! 11 a5! ♘bd7 12 cxd5 exd5 13 a6! with a large white advantage. Black should have played 10...a5 to prevent the advance of the a-pawn.

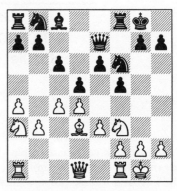

10 ...   ♘e4

Yusupov suggested 10...♗d7.

11 ♘c2   ♘d7

The immediate 11...a5 is also good, for example 12 ♘e5 ♘d7 13 f4 ♘xe5 14 dxe5 ♘c5 15 ♘d4 ♗d7 16 ♖c1 ♘xd3 17 ♕xd3 c5 18 ♘e2 ♗c6 19 ♘c3 dxc4 20 ♕xc4 ♖ad8 with equality, Torrecillas-Illescas Cordoba, Spain 1991.

12 ♕e1   a5
13 ♘d2   b6
14 f3   ♘xd2

| 15 | ♕xd2 | ♘f6 |

On 15...♗b7 follows 16 e4.

16	♖fd1	♗a6
17	♘e1!	♖fc8
18	♖ac1	♕b7
19	♕f2?!	

White should continue with 19 ♗f1 to complete the manoeuvre ♘c2-e1-d3-e5.

19	...	c5!
20	♕g3	cxd4
21	exd4	dxc4
22	bxc4	♕c7
23	♗f1	♕xg3
24	hxg3	♖a7?

Black wants to put the pawn on c4 under heavy pressure by means of ...♖ac7, but this allows the white knight to improve its position. Black should have executed his plan starting with 24...♖c6.

25	♘c2!	♖ac7
26	♘a3	♘d5
27	♖e1	♔f7
28	♖e5	♘b4
29	♖ce1	

Now it is Black who is feeling the pressure.

29	...	♖c6
30	♘b5	♗xb5
31	axb5	♖d6
32	c5	♖xd4
33	cxb6	♖d6
34	b7	♖b8
35	♗c4	♔f8

Black can no longer defend e6, as 35...♘d5 fails to 36 ♖xe6!

36	♗xe6	♖xb7
37	♖xf5+	♔e8
38	♗d7++?	

This looks strong, but much better was 38 ♗g8+ with good winning chances. After the time-trouble induced text move Yusupov escapes with a draw.

| 38 | ... | ♔d8 |

Certainly not 38...♔xd7 39 ♖f7+ ♔c8 40 ♖e8+.

39	♖f8+	♔c7
40	♗c8	♖b8
41	♖f7+	♔b6

41...♔xc8? 42 ♖c1+ wins.

42	♗f5	♖f6
43	♖xf6+	gxf6
44	♗xh7	a4
45	♖a1	♖a8

46	♗e4	♖a7
47	♖a3	♔xb5
48	♔f2	♘a6
49	g4	♘c5
50	♗d5	♖d7
51	♗g8	♔b4
52	♖e3	♖d8

½-½

The setup with 3 ♘f3 and 4 ♕c2 is popular among positional players and Game 46 shows this setup with a fianchetto on the kingside. Black has good chances in this variation; in most cases it is White who has to fight for an equal position.

Game 46
Urday – Tregubov
Berlin open 1995

1	d4	d5
2	♘f3	c6
3	c4	e6
4	♕c2	♘f6

This is Black's best choice, unless he wishes to switch to a main line Stonewall Dutch after 4...f5 5 g3. Both 4...♗d6 and 4...dxc4 are inferior. Two terrifying examples:
- 4...♗d6 5 ♗g5 ♘e7 6 e3 ♘d7 7 ♘c3 h6 8 ♗h4 dxc4 9 ♗xc4 0-0 10 0-0-0 ♖e8 11 g4 ♘f8 12 ♘e4 ♗c7 13 ♗g3 ♗xg3 14 hxg3 f6 15 ♘xf6+! gxf6 16 ♖xh6 ♘d5 17 ♖dh1 f5 18 ♘e5 b5 19 f4 1-0, Magerramov-Zaitseva, Moscow 1992
- 4...dxc4 5 ♕xc4 b5 6 ♕c2 ♗b7 7 e4 ♘d7 8 ♘c3 ♖c8 9 a3 ♘e7?! (9...♘gf6 is natural) 10 ♗e3 ♘g6 11 ♗e2 a6 12 0-0 c5 13 d5 ♕c7 14 dxe6 fxe6 15 ♘g5 ♕c6 16 ♗g4 b4 17 ♘a4 ♘f6 18 ♗xe6 ♖c7 19 ♖ad1 ♗d6 20 ♗d5 ♘xd5 21 exd5 ♕b5 22 ♘e6 1-0, Stohl-Knaak, Stara Zagora zonal 1990.

5 g3
Apart from 5 ♗g5, which we discuss in the next game, and 5 e3 ♘bd7 6 ♘c3 transposing to the Meran Defence, White can also play 5 ♘bd2. Black's easiest way to equalize is 5...dxc4. In Stohl-Matlak, Czech Republic 1994, matters quickly simplified after 6 ♘xc4 c5 7 dxc5 ♗xc5 8 a3 0-0 9 b4 ♗e7 10 ♗b2 ♘bd7 11 ♘d4 ♕c7 12 ♖c1 ♘b6 13 ♘a5 ♕xc2 14 ♖xc2 ♘a4 15 ♗a1 ♘d5.

5	...	dxc4
6	♕xc4	b5 *(D)*
7	♕d3	

A more common continuation is 7 ♕c2 ♗b7, when White has two alternatives:
- 8 ♘bd2. In the game Akesson-Maksimenko, Farum 1993, Black had a clear plus after 8...♘bd7 9 ♘b3 ♕b6 10 ♗g2 a5 11 a4 ♗b4+ 12 ♗d2 bxa4 13 ♖xa4 ♕b5 14 ♖a1 a4 15 ♘c1 c5. Better is 9 e4 ♗e7 10 a3 followed by 11 b4, an

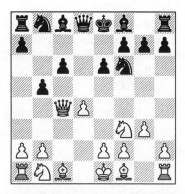

interesting plan from M.Gurevich-R.Kuijf, Belgium 1996. Instead of 10...♕b6 11 b4 a5 12 ♖b1 with some advantage for White, Black can prevent 11 b4 with 10...a5 or make a promising pawn sacrifice with 10...c5 11 ♗b5 0-0, when the combination of ♗b5 and g3 looks rather odd.

• 8 ♗g2, when the game Berezin-R.Kuijf, Groningen 1995, shows the ideal strategy for Black: 8...♘bd7 9 0-0 c5 10 dxc5 ♗xc5 11 ♘c3 ♖c8 12 ♕d3 a6 13 a3 0-0 14 ♗g5 h6 15 ♗f4 ♘b6 16 ♖ad1 ♕xd3 17 ♖xd3 ♘c4 18 ♗c1 ♖fd8 19 ♘e1 ♗xg2 20 ♔xg2 ♗d4 21 ♘f3 ♗xc3 22 ♖xc3 ♘e4 23 ♖d3 ♘c5 24 ♖c3 ♘a4 25 ♖b3 ♘a5 26 ♖b4 ♖c4 27 ♗d2 ♖xb4 28 axb4 ♘b3 29 ♗c3 f6 30 h4 h5 31 ♔h3 ♔f7 32 g4 hxg4+ 33 ♔xg4 ♖c8 34 ♖d1 ♘xc3 35 bxc3 ♖xc3 36 ♖d7+ ♔g6 37 ♖d6 ♖c4+ 38 ♔g3 ♖xb4 39 ♖xa6 ♘c5 40 ♖c6 ♖c4 41 ♔g2 b4 42 e3 b3 43 ♖b6 ♖c3 44 ♖b5 ♘d3 45 h5+ ♔h7 46 ♖b8 b2 47 ♘h4 ♖c8 48 ♖xc8 b1♕ 0-1.

7 ...	♗b7
8 ♗g2	♘bd7
9 0-0	a6
10 a4	

A better way to prevent 10...c5 is 10 ♘g5 ♕b6 11 ♘c3 ♖d8, as in Sakaev-Maksimenko, Tivat 1995. However, apparently White did not see any advantage, because the game ended in a draw here.

10 ... c5

This is clearly sufficient for a good position. A solid alternative is 10...♗e7 11 ♘bd2 0-0 12 b3 ♕b6 13 e4 c5 14 ♗a3 h6 15 ♖fe1 ♖fe8 with an equal position in Grabliauskas-Makarov, Lyon 1994.

| 11 axb5 | ♗e4 |
| 12 ♕d1 | |

In the game Tukmakov-Kharlov, Bern 1992, Black was better after 12 ♕b3 ♗d5 13 ♕c2 axb5 14 ♖xa8 ♕xa8 15 ♘c3 ♗c6 16 e4 ♘xe4 17 dxc5 ♘xc3 18 ♕xc3 b4 19 ♕b3 ♗xc5.

12 ...	axb5
13 ♖xa8	♕xa8
14 ♘c3	

The game Wojtkiewicz-Matlak, Wizla 1992, ended in a draw after 14 ♗g5 cxd4 15 ♗xf6 ♘xf6 16 ♕xd4 ♗e7 17 ♘c3 ♗c6 18 ♘h4 ♗xg2 19 ♘xg2 b4 20 ♘b5 0-0 21 ♕a7 ♕d5 22 ♕xe7 ♕xb5 23 ♘f4 e5 24 ♘d3 e4 25 ♕xb4 ♖b8 26 ♕xb5 ♖xb5 27 ♖c1 ♔f8 28 ♘f4.

| 14 ... | ♗c6 |
| 15 ♘h4?! | |

White's best option was to play for a draw with 15 dxc5.

| 15 ... | ♗xg2 |

16	♘xg2	b4
17	♘b5	♕c6
18	♕a4	♗e7
19	dxc5	0-0
20	♗e3	

20 ♘c3?! ♕xc5 21 ♗e3 ♕e5 22 ♘d1 ♘c5 23 ♕c2 ♖d8 24 ♗f4 ♕e4 is clearly better for Black, Korsunsky-Maksimenko, Ukraine 1992, and 20 ♕xb4? loses a knight after 20...♗xc5! 21 ♕a4 ♖a8 22 ♕b3 ♖b8 23 ♘d4 ♕e4.

20	...	♗xc5
21	♘c3	♕b7
22	♕b5	♕a8!

White has got rid of the pin, but he still has problems, for instance 23 ♗xc5 ♖b8 24 ♕c4 bxc3 25 b4 ♘e4 26 ♗e3 ♖c8 and Black is better.

23	♘d1	♖b8
24	♕c4	♗f8

White's pieces lack coordination, so Black avoids the exchange of bishops.

25	♘f4	♖c8
26	♕b3	e5
27	♘d3	♕d5

28	♕a4	

Equally unpleasant for White is 28 ♕xd5 ♘xd5 followed by ...♖c2.

28	...	h5
29	♗d2	♘c5
30	♕c2	

30 ♕b5 ♘xd3 31 ♕xd5 ♘xd5 32 exd3 ♖c2 is a wonderful endgame for Black.

30	...	♕e6

A strong option is 30...♕d8 intending 31 ♕b1 ♘xd3 32 exd3 e4.

31	♘e3	

Black has a winning position after 31 ♘xb4 ♘b3 32 ♕d3 e4 33 ♕e3 ♘g4 34 ♕f4 ♗d6 35 ♕g5 f6 or 31 ♘xc5 ♗xc5 32 ♕d3 e4 followed by ...♕h3 and ...♘g4.

31	...	♘b3
32	♕d1	♖d8

33	f3	

White cannot prevent 33...♘xd2 and 34...e4 since 33 ♗e1 loses to 33...e4 34 ♘f4 ♖xd1 35 ♘xe6 ♖xe1 36 ♖xe1 fxe6 37 ♖d1 ♗e7.

33	...	♘xd2
34	♕xd2	e4
35	fxe4	♘xe4

36 ♕e1 ♛b6 37 ♕c1 ♖e8 38 ♔g2 ♘g5?! (38...♘xg3 wins a pawn under even better conditions) 39 ♘d5 ♖xe2+ 40 ♖f2 ♖xf2+ 41 ♘xf2 ♛d8 42 ♕c4 ♛a8 43 h4 ♘e6 44 ♘e4 ♛b8 45 b3 ♔h8 46 ♔h3? (if White wants to move his king it should be to h2. However, Black now overlooks the winning manoeuvre 46...♛a7! 47 ♔g2 ♛a2+ 48 ♔h3 ♛b1 49 ♔g2 ♛e1 followed by ...f7-f5 and ...♗c5) 46...♛e5? 47 ♘xb4 f5 48 ♘f2 ♗d6 49 ♔g2 ♛xg3+ 50 ♔f1 ♛e3? (this throws the advantage away. Black is still better after the obvious 50...♗c5

51 ♘bd3 ♗xf2 52 ♘xf2 ♛e5 53 b4 ♘d4) 51 ♘d5 ♛e5 52 b4 (now White's b-pawn starts to count, so Black must satisfy himself with a draw) 52...♔h7 53 b5 ♗c5 54 ♘d3 ♛a1+ 55 ♔e2 ♘d4+ 56 ♔f2 ♗d6 57 b6 ♗h2 58 ♔e3 ♗g1+ 59 ♔d2 ♘f3+ 60 ♔e2 ♘d4+ 61 ♔d2 ♘f3+ ½-½

A better way for White to try for an advantage is 4 ♕c2 ♘f6 5 ♗g5. The following game is a disaster for Black but he should still be able to achieve an acceptable position.

Game 47
C.Horvath – R.Kuijf
Bad Wörishofen open 1993

1 d4	d5
2 c4	e6
3 ♘f3	c6
4 ♕c2	♘f6
5 ♗g5	♘bd7

5...♛a5+ is the main alternative. In Kholmov-Nei, Tbilisi 1966 Black had an equal position after 6 ♗d2 ♛d8 7 e3 ♘bd7 8 ♘c3 c5 9 cxd5 exd5 10 ♗e2 ♗e7 11 0-0 0-0. Another plan originates from Brunner-Stangl, Germany 1995, in which Black had no problems after the opening: 5...dxc4 6 ♕xc4 b5 7 ♕c2 ♗b7 8 ♘c3 ♘bd7 9 e3 a6 10 ♗e2 c5 11 dxc5 ♗xc5 12 0-0 ♖c8 13 ♖fd1 ♛c7 14 ♖ac1 0-0.

6 e3	♛a5+
7 ♘bd2	

7 ♘c3 leads to the Cambridge Springs variation of the Queen's Gambit, which is outside the scope of this book.

7 ...	♘e4
8 ♗f4	♗b4
9 a3	g5?!

In the game Korchnoi-Godena, Debrecen 1992, Black played 9...f5 but failed to achieve full equality after 10 ♖d1 ♗d6 11 ♗d3 h6 12 0-0 g5 13 ♗g3 ♘xg3 14 hxg3 ♘f6 15 ♖c1 ♗d7 16 ♘b3, though the game ended in a draw. However, the consequences of 9...g5 seem to favour White.

10 ♗g3	h5

This is clearly better than 10...g4 11 ♖d1!, as played in the game

Davies-Manor, Tel-Aviv 1988. Black resigned after 11...♗e7 12 ♘e5 ♘xg3 13 hxg3 ♘xe5 14 dxe5 h5 15 ♗e2 ♗d7 16 ♗xg4 dxc4 17 ♖xh5 ♖xh5 18 ♗xh5 0-0-0 19 ♗xf7 ♕c5 20 ♕c3 ♕d5 21 e4 ♕c5 22 ♘xc4 1-0.

11 0-0-0

11 ...   ♗e7?

Much better is 11...♗xa3! 12 bxa3 ♕xa3+ 13 ♕b2 ♕xb2+ 14 ♔xb2 h4 15 ♘xe4 dxe4 16 ♗d6! exf3 17 gxf3 f6 18 ♖g1 ♔f7 19 ♗e2 and although White has the better prospects Black is still fighting, Khalifman-Van der Werf, Wijk aan Zee 1995.

12 ♘xe4   dxe4
13 ♕xe4   h4
14 ♗e5   f6

Is Black winning a piece?

15 ♕g6+   ♔f8
16 d5!

No, but White is winning the game!

16 ...   cxd5
17 ♗c3   ♕c7
18 ♘xg5   1-0

Index of Variations

(reference numbers refer to page numbers)

7...♗b7
    8 axb5 ♗xc3 9 ♘xc3 cxb5
        10 b3 a5   main line (see below – 7...a5 8 axb5 ♗xc3
                          9 ♘xc3 cxb5 10 b3 ♗b7)
        10 d5   *56*
    8 ♘e5   *47*
    8 b3   *51*
7...♕e7   *44*
7...♕b6   *44*
8 axb5
8 ♘e5   *47*
8 ♖b1   *49*
8 ♕b1   *49*
8 ♕c2   *50*
8...♗xc3 9 ♘xc3 cxb5 10 b3
10 ♕b1   *54*
10 ♘e5   *54*
10 d5   *58*
10...♗b7 11 bxc4
11 d5 ♘f6
    12 dxe6   *58*
    12 bxc4 b4
        13 ♕a4+   *59*
        13 ♗xf6 ♕xf6 14 ♕a4+ ♘d7 15 ♘d4 e5 16 ♘b3 ♔e7
                17 ♕b5   *59*
                17 e4   *59*
                17 ♖d1   *59*
                17 ♗e2   *60*
11...b4 12 ♗b2
12 ♗d2   *62*
12...♘f6 13 ♗d3
13 c5   *63*
13 ♗e2   *63*
13...♘bd7
13...♗e4   *65*
14 0-0
14 ♕c2
    14...♕c7
        15 0-0 0-0 main line (see below – 14 0-0 0-0
                       15 ♕c2 ♕c7)
        15 e4 e5
             16 0-0 0-0 main line (see below – 14 0-0 0-0
                       15 ♕c2 ♕c7 16 e4 e5)
             16 dxe5   *65*
    14...0-0   *65*
14...0-0

14...♛c7
       15 ♕c2 0-0 main line (14...0-0 15 ♕c2 ♕c7)
       15 ♖e1 0-0
              16 e4   *66*
              16 c5   *66*
     15 ♘d2 e5
              16 ♖e1   *68*
              16 f3   *68*
              16 f4   *71*
              16 dxe5 *71*
     15 d5   *72*

15 ♕c2
15 ♘d2   *73*
15...♕c7 16 e4
16 c5   *75*
16 ♘e5   *77*
16 ♖fe1 ♖fe8
       17 e4 e5 main line (see below – 16 e4 e5 17 ♖fe1 ♖fe8)
       17 ♘e5   *77*
16...e5 17 ♖fe1
17 ♘xe5 *79*
17 d5   *79*
17 h3   *79*
17 c5
       17...exd4 *81*
       17...♖fe8 *81*
       17...♗a6   *81*
       17...h6   *83*
17...♖fe8 18 c5
18 dxe5   *85*
18...exd4
18...♗a6   *85*
18...h6   *85*
19 ♗xd4 h6
19...♘g4   *85*
19...♗a6   *85*
20 e5
20 h3   *85*
20...♘d5 21 e6
21 ♗e4   *87*
21...♖xe6 22 ♖xe6 fxe6 23 ♖e1 ♘f4 24.♗e4 ♖c8 25 g3
25 ♘e5   *87*
25...♘h3+
26 ♔f1   *89*
26 ♔g2   *89*

Anti-Noteboom systems

1 d4 d5 2 c4 e6 3 ♘c3
        3 ♘f3 c6
                4 ♘c3   Noteboom variation
                4 e3   *117*
                4 ♕c2 ♘f6
                        4...dxc4   *120*
                        4...♗d6   *120*
                5 e3   *120*
                5 g3   *120*
                5 ♘bd2 *120*
                5 ♗g5   *123*

3...c6 4 e4
                4 ♘f3   Noteboom variation
                4 cxd5 exd5
                        5 ♗f4   *105*
                        5 ♕c2   *105*
                        5 ♘f3   *108*
            4 ♗f4   *112*
            4 e3   *114*

4...dxe4
                4...♗b4   *102*

5 ♘xe4 ♗b4+ 6 ♗d2
            6 ♘c3   *91*

6...♕xd4 7 ♗xb4 ♕xe4+ 8 ♗e2
            8 ♘e2   *100*

8...c5
                8...♘a6   *92*
                8...♘d7   *92*
                8...♘e7   *92*

9 ♗xc5   *95*
9 ♗c3   *97*